BELLEVUE AND THE NEW EASTSIDE

"Eastside Enterprises" by D.Ann Slayton Shiffler

Produced in cooperation with the
Bellevue Chamber of Commerce

Windsor Publications, Inc.
Chatsworth, California

BELLEVUE

EASTSIDE

AND THE NEW

A CONTEMPORARY PORTRAIT BY BOB WELCH

Windsor Publications, Inc.—Book Division
Managing Editor: **Karen Story**
Design Director: **Alexander D'Anca**
Photo Director: **Susan L. Wells**
Executive Editor: **Pamela Schroeder**

Staff for *Bellevue and the New Eastside*
Manuscript Editor: **Kevin Taylor**
Photo Editors: **Cameron Cox, Teri Greenberg**
Production Editor, Text: **Doreen Nakakihara**
Senior Editor, Corporate Profiles: **Judith L. Hunter**
Production Editor, Corporate Profiles: **Albert Polito**
Customer Service Manager: **Phyllis Feldman-Schroeder**
Editorial Assistants: **Kim Kievman, Michael Nugwynne, Michele Oakley,**
Kathy B. Peyser, Susan Schlanger, Theresa J. Solis
Publisher's Representatives, Corporate Profiles: **David B. Cook,**
Elizabeth A. Cook
Layout Artist, Corporate Profiles: **Bonnie Felt**
Production Assistant: **Deena Tucker**
Designer: **Christina L. Rosepapa**

Library of Congress Cataloging-in-Publication Data

Welch, Bob, 1954-
Bellevue and the new Eastside: a contemporary portrait/by Bob Welch.
p. 208   cm. 23x31
Includes bibliographical references.
ISBN 0-89781-331-6
1. Bellevue (Wash.)—Description. 2. Bellevue (Wash.)—Economic conditions.
3. Bellevue (Wash.)—Industries.   4. Eastside (Wash.)—Description and travel.
5. Eastside (Wash.)—Economic conditions.   6. Eastside (Wash.)—Industries   I. Title
F899. B39W45   1989
979.7'77—dc20   89-22684
                                                              CIP

Windsor Publications, Inc.
Elliot Martin, Chairman of the Board
James L. Fish III, Chief Operating Officer
Michele Sylvestro, Vice President/Sales-Marketing

Title spread: The warm glow of a Washington sunset silhouettes the changing face of downtown Bellevue. Photo by Eric Draper

Facing page: The rich colors of an Eastside sunset highlight the tranquil waters of Lake Washington. Photo by Gary Greene

To the people who live, work,
and play on the Eastside

CONTENTS

The Bellevue Metro Transit Center stands out against the familiar facade of the Koll Center. Photo by Wolfgang Kaehler

ACKNOWLEDGMENTS

I'd like to thank Robert Hartley, vice president of The Rockey Company, for his editing and encouragement; *The Journal American*, for allowing me access to its excellent library; my two sons, Ryan and Jason, for understanding why Dad had taken up permanent residence in front of the home computer; and my wife, Sally, for not only understanding, but leaving occasional packs of Lifesavers by the keyboard.

FOREWORD

It's not often in today's world that we can participate in the development of a new city—a city where standards for quality of life and economic vitality are exceptional by any measure.

Our new "city"—the Eastside—is really several cities. Each city on the Eastside offers unique services and employment and business opportunities. Each has its own ambience. Together the cities form a sophisticated business and residential center for Puget Sound.

Bellevue and the New Eastside is our way of celebrating the new city. The chapters inside describe slices of Eastside life we experience every day, but the words are still a delightful surprise. Thriving businesses and diverse employment opportunities. Astonishing natural beauty. Unsurpassed community amenities. No wonder we look at our home with pride.

History has shown that the early residents of Bellevue and its environs had a unique vision of its future, and their vision resulted in a prosperous, caring community. The Bellevue Chamber of Commerce shared their vision then and still does today. We work for enhanced economic development and quality of life. We strive for excellent schools and adequate resources to meet human service needs.

Meeting the community's needs is a growth challenge faced by Bellevue and the Eastside. Those needs will be met because this Chamber, as well as other organizations, thinks regionally. We see coalition-building as our key to success. We're proud of our "city," and working with others toward common goals is the most productive way to show it.

The exciting images in the pages ahead will make you proud of the Eastside, as we are. Celebrate with us the development of our new city!

Dickwin D. Armstrong
President
Bellevue Chamber of Commerce

These small boats are chained together on a dock in the waterfront community of Medina. Photo by Gary Greene

FLYING HIGH ON THE EASTSIDE

A kaleidoscope of color trans-
forms the sky over the Sammamish Valley as balloons
take to the sky. Photo by
Gary Greene

1
SETTING THE STAGE

As the northbound Boeing 747-400 banks hard right shortly after its takeoff from Seattle's Sea-Tac International Airport, you see it below—an area that stretches along the eastern shores of Lake Washington, blue-gray water wrapped around forested fingers of land. An area framed by the 18-mile-long lake and the jagged peaks of the Cascades, cloaked in their wintry white. An area where fir trees and parks and neighborhoods surround the municipal hub, downtown Bellevue, its new buildings a symbolic salute to a region on the rise.

This is Bellevue and the Eastside, Washington's rising star. From the air it unfolds like a chamber of commerce president's dream, a mosaic of mountains, water, and trees. Some describe this enticing slice of the Pacific Northwest in paradisiacal terms. It offers a thriving business environment, a downtown that's gained national attention, well-planned, wooded neighborhoods, schools that rank among the state's best, first-class cultural opportunities, and more outdoor activities than some entire states offer.

Paradise? No. Such a place does not exist. But some, even those who have lived in many places around the country, will tell you it may be as close as you can get. As the state of Washington celebrates its centennial anniversary in 1989, the Eastside has emerged as a shining example of the best of both worlds: work and play.

To understand this place, you must understand the variety it offers in both realms. The Eastside is a board meeting on the 25th floor of a

The sun sets on the
peaceful waters of
Lake Washington.
Photo by Gary
Greene

Above: Boats remain a popular form of transportation for area residents. Photo by Gary Greene

Facing page: A small group of local fishermen try their luck in the rich waters of Lake Washington. Photo by Gary Greene

Bellevue high rise, Mount Rainier standing watch from afar. And a 24-foot San Juan sailboat, only a mile from that high rise, slicing across Meydenbauer Bay.

The Eastside is two software engineers brainstorming over a program change at Redmond's Evergreen Place Business Park. And two music lovers listening to the Bellevue Philharmonic play Mozart's Symphony No. 40 in G minor.

It's a Carnation farmer guiding his cows into the barn for an early-morning milking. And three fitness buffs waving to that farmer as they glide by for some early-morning cycling.

Right: This pastoral scene is commonplace in Woodinville, which has more horses per capita than any other Washington community. Photo by Eric Draper

Below: The majestic Cascades lend their splendor and diversity to the region outlying Bellevue. Photo by Gary Greene

It's an open-heart surgery at Bellevue's Overlake Hospital Medical Center. And a frog-jumping contest at the annual Duvall Days Country Livin' Festival.

It's the Seattle Seahawks football team running wind sprints at its Kirkland headquarters, an early-autumn sun sinking lower across Lake Washington. And two neighbors in the new Klahanie neighborhood stopping their lawn work to chat, starting out on the subject of weeds and finishing up with plans for a two-family barbecue.

It's a floatplane taking off from Lake Washington with two businessmen

headed for Vancouver, British Columbia. And thousands of sun-drenched people enjoying a seemingly endless display of arts and crafts at the Pacific Northwest Arts & Crafts Fair.

It's a semi-truck rolling down Interstate 405 with a 747 engine on its trailer. And, less than a mile away, in a dense thicket in 482-acre Bridle State Park, a rider on horseback enjoying the silence of the woods.

It's two high-powered CEOs doing business over lunch at The Lakes Club atop the 25-story Security Pacific Plaza. And 200 low-key teenagers sunbathing and playing volleyball at Kirkland's Houghton Park on Lake Washington.

It's a volunteer at Bellevue's Merrywood School teaching a disabled child to walk. And representatives from the city of Redmond sketching plans for the 1990 Goodwill Games, whose bicycle races will be on the Eastside.

It's a 12-year-old boy delivering the Eastside's daily newspaper, *The Journal American*. And an 85-year-old woman swimming laps at Pacific Regent's glass-enclosed pool, "The Cocoon," before heading to the dining room for chicken fettuccine ricardo.

It's a Vietnamese refugee learning how to fill out a tax form at Bellevue's Eastside Resettlement Center. And two dozen rambunctious preschoolers frolicking on a rubber boat at Bellevue Square, their not-so-rambunctious parents wondering if the kids' batteries ever run low.

Above all, the Eastside is a place where the living, working, and playing blend into a quality of life so attractive that the area is growing at more than twice the national average. Though not without its struggles, the region has maintained much of the charm and luster that drew people here in the first place.

The annual Derby Days event in Redmond features a spectacular bike race for those with a thirst for competition. Photo by Eric Draper

juried art exhibit
at bellevue art museum

U.S. BANK
Unbeatable

The annual Pacific North-west Arts and Crafts Fair draws thousands of residents during the last week in July. Photo by Gary Greene

Defining the Eastside

If you were sitting in that Boeing 747-400 and looking at the Eastside, you wouldn't see any distinct boundaries that define this region, other than Lake Washington at the western edge. Just east of Seattle, across the lake, the Eastside is roughly a 20-mile-by-20-mile area that stretches north to Bothell, south to Bellevue, and east to North Bend in the foothills of the Cascades. It is home to some 350,000 people.

Bellevue, sandwiched between Lake Washington and Lake Sammamish, is the Eastside's flagship city. With a population of 82,070, it is King County's second largest city and the state's fourth largest, which is amazing considering it is among the Northwest's younger cities, having not incorporated until 1953. But what it has lacked in time, it has made up for in planning, work, and pride. The result is a downtown that has gained national acclaim for its architecture. That has become the center of a business setting which offers more commercial office space than the Portland central business district. That is home to an upscale shopping center, Bellevue Square, that drew 11.5 million shoppers in 1987.

"Of all America's big suburbs turned cities, Bellevue seems to be making the most conscious pitch for quality," wrote Neal R. Peirce, the *Washington Post* writer, syndicated columnist, and coauthor of *The Book of America*. People looking for places to live and work are attracted to that quality; between 1980 and 1987, no other Washington city added more people to its census rolls than Bellevue: 8,167.

Left: The shoreline of Lake Sammamish State Park provides the setting for this peaceful image. Photo by Gary Greene

Clyde Hill and the waterfront communities of Beaux Arts, Medina, Hunts Point, and Yarrow Point flank Bellevue to the east. The waterfront area is sprinkled with plush homes hidden away in the trees, some in the million-dollar range. Lush, green lawns surround the houses and wrap around tennis courts and pools. Out back, lavish boats and an occasional floatplane bob on Lake Washington. The five communities, with a combined population of about 7,500, not only are the wealthiest communities on the Eastside but in the state as well. In 1985 Hunts Point had a per capita income of $49,380, followed by Medina at $28,600, Yarrow Point at $24,900, Clyde Hill at $24,820, and Beaux Arts at $23,820. (The average per capita income on the Eastside is $17,575.)

North along Lake Washington sits Kirkland, a mostly residential community with four miles of waterfront. The 1988 incorporation of the Rose Hill area boosted Kirkland's population to 35,823, making it the state's 11th largest city. Carillon Point, a new waterfront development that includes a marina, restaurant, and office/retail space, gives the city another dash of class. Despite such growth, Kirkland has maintained a charm that many cities its size have lost. A 1988 *Sunset* magazine article described Kirkland as "still a friendly village," with a waterfront downtown boasting a perfect blend of "old-fashioned local service stores side-by-side with trendy new restaurants and shops."

Redmond sits to the east of Kirkland, just north of Lake Sammamish's upper reaches. The state's fastest-growing city from 1970 to 1980, Redmond (population 31,000) is headquarters for high-tech giants Microsoft and Nintendo, both world leaders in their fields. But Redmond is much more than business. It's the bicycle capital of the Northwest, and in the summer, morning and evening skies are dotted with hot-air balloons gliding high over the Sammamish Valley. The city is particularly popular with families; many are attracted to its numerous wooded homesites.

To the north, the Bothell-North Creek area is the gateway to The Technology

Corridor along Interstate 405. A mixture of old and new, Bothell has a population of 8,825. Mill Creek, with a population of 4,338, is a new community whose focus is the Mill Creek Country Club. Unincorporated Woodinville (population 19,000) draws its residents mainly because of its country feel, though its business climate nurtures several wineries and Molbak's, a world-class greenhouse. Woodinville has more horses per capita than any other community in Washington, offering true "country living, city style."

The eastern portion of the Eastside is largely open space; cows nonchalantly chew grass near small towns such as Duvall and Carnation. The lower Snoqualmie Valley is the center of King County's dairy industry, but, even so, much of the area's growth is headed in that direction. The East Sammamish area (unincorporated King County land east of Lake Sammamish) grew at more than twice the rate of the rest of the Eastside during the 1980s.

In 1981 Issaquah, located at the south end of Lake Sammamish, had one traffic signal. By the end of the decade it had five signals, with 27 scheduled to be installed by 1993. The Issaquah post office ranks as one of the three fastest growing in the state, along with Redmond's and Woodinville's, and the city's population has risen to 7,100. Issaquah sits at the foot of the "Issaquah Alps," where hikers can break a sweat within minutes of leaving their houses. Home of one of the state's best salmon-spawning streams, Issaquah puts on a weekend Salmon Days festival each fall that is regarded among the state's best civic celebrations. Further east, the communities of North Bend, Fall City, and Snoqualmie exude a country feel, the Cascades towering in their backyards and Snoqualmie Falls plummeting nearby.

Above: A familiar sight now to Bellevue residents are the colorful hot-air balloons that dot the skies of the Sammamish Valley. Photo by Eric Draper

Facing page: At twilight a sailboat docks at Kirkland on Lake Washington. Photo by Gary Greene

Climate

Those unfamiliar with the Northwest need only one word to describe the region's climate: Wet. Those who do live here know better. None would deny that the region gets its share of rain; in fact, Eastsiders can expect 34.1 inches of rain per year. But Eastsiders are quick to point out that they get less rain per year than people in New

York City, Philadelphia, Washington, D.C., and Memphis, among other places. Summers are relatively rain-free; the average July rainfall, for example, is just over half an inch. Rather than call their climate "wet," they would rather call it "mild." Or even "diverse." Eastsiders experience a little bit of all sorts of weather, but rarely must endure the hot spells and cold snaps that grip other U.S. regions.

The Puget Sound area has a mild, marine, West Coast clime. On average, the area will get three days a year when temperatures rise to 90 degrees or above and 31 days when the mercury falls to freezing or below. While Seattle has experienced highs to 100 and lows to zero, summer afternoons are typically 70 to 80 degrees. Eastside nights will drop into the 50s, meaning air-conditioning is seldom needed. Winter temperatures generally linger in the 40s. Summers are pleasant; 70 percent of Seattle's clear skies will come between May 1 and October 31.

While Eastside weather is generally predictable, there are enough exceptions to keep things interesting. Back-to-back storms in November 1985 unleashed 17.4 inches of snow on Seattle. In 1987 a regional drought forced Eastside city governments to mandate a cutback on water use. In February 1989 a record-setting cold snap sent temperatures into single digits; a surprise March snowfall a month later buried the Eastside in up to a foot of the white stuff.

When spring arrives, the lushness of the trees and plants seems to make the wet and cold of winter seem worthwhile, each drop of rain meaning that the summer garden will do all the better.

Speaking of Growth . . .

In 1928, when one of Bellevue's first developers, James S. Ditty, predicted a day when some 200,000 people would live on the Eastside, people laughed. Now with nearly twice that many people, the Eastside has blossomed like few believed it would. Since 1964 Seattle's population has slipped from 564,000 to 491,300, a decrease of 13 percent. In the same time period, Redmond's population has grown ten-fold, Bellevue's sixfold, and Kirkland's threefold.

"Growth on the Eastside was way more than people anticipated," said Albert D. Rosellini, former governor of Washington, in celebrating the 25th anniversary of the Evergreen Point Floating Bridge in 1988. When the bridge was built in 1963, some predicted 15,000 cars a day would use it. Today more than 100,000 vehicles use it daily and another 65,000 use the Mercer Island Floating Bridge, the Eastside's other link to Seattle.

On the Eastside it is not uncommon to drive by a construction site where a dozen houses are in progress, at least one of which has a plywood board spray-painted with a message: "Framers Needed." Eighty-five percent of new construction in King County during the 1980s was on the Eastside, according to Bellevue-based Hebert Research Inc., a company that tracks the Puget Sound region statistically.

The lower Snoqualmie Valley is the center of King County's dairy industry. These cows were photographed in the community of Duvall. Photo by Gary Greene

Boeing has long been the Eastside's economic stabilizer; some 12,000 Eastsiders, one in 12 employed adults, work for the world's aerospace leader. But two other things have fueled the area's surge in the 1980s: the growth of the high-tech industry—the Eastside is the state's high-tech hotbed—and the emergence of downtown Bellevue as a first-class place to do business.

One in four Eastsiders now works directly or indirectly for high-tech firms, and the growth of high tech and other industries has brought expansion to downtown Bellevue. The 1980s saw a lackluster downtown Bellevue turn into a major-league downtown. From 1981 to 1987 a handful of new high rises helped office space grow 66 percent. Bellevue Square's successful redevelopment thrust the mall among the nation's elite. And the aesthetics of the downtown area, enhanced by a new park, have drawn praise from the national press and urban design experts. "The city has an absolutely outstanding planning and urban design program," said *USA Today* in 1988.

Such growth and attention have made comparisons between Bellevue and Seattle inevitable, but Eastside civic leaders agree that no rivalry exists between the two. Despite the Eastside's gains, Seattle remains Washington's financial and

The Evergreen Point Floating Bridge, which was 25 years old in 1988, has more than 100,000 vehicles travel across it daily. Photo by Gary Greene

cultural center, a gateway to thriving Pacific Rim trade. "Our relationship is symbiotic," said Kemper Freeman, Jr., who helped develop Bellevue Square, developed Bellevue Place, and served for a time as chairman of the Bellevue Chamber of Commerce. "If things are going well in Seattle, things are going well over here."

In 1987 *The Journal American* said that cooperation, not competitiveness, is needed between the two. "If we are looking for competitors," said *The J-A*, "they are Portland, San Francisco, or Los Angeles, not close neighbors."

Quality of Life

In 1988 a 34-year-old Beverly Hills woman grew tired of the Los Angeles area, tired of traffic and smog and a rising crime rate. So she decided to move. She considered four areas—Scottsdale, San Diego, San Francisco, and Bellevue. She chose the latter. "Every time I go across the bridge to Seattle I think of how good it is to see nature all around me—the water, mountains, trees—instead of concrete buildings," said Sharon Franz. "It's natural tranquility."

The Eastside's attraction is a quality of life that exists for a myriad of reasons, ranging from the environment to a relatively low crime rate. "People who live here all the time think it's normal," said Kemper Freeman. "But people visiting from other places come to Bellevue and say, 'My gosh, what's going on here? The place is clean. It's alive with people. And everyone seems to have a job.'" In 1988 Eastside employment was growing at a rate of 3.75 percent per year, compared to 1.25 percent in Seattle.

For people like Sharon Franz, Eastside real estate is a bargain. In 1988 the average price of a house in California was $160,073; in King County the average was $108,000. That same year, Linda and Jan Brandon of San Jose sold the family's 1,000-square-foot bungalow for $191,000 and moved to the Sammamish Plateau, where they paid $154,000 for a 2,500-square-foot, four-bedroom, three-car-garage house among the trees.

Other economic advantages exist. Of the major western cities, Seattle's cost-of-living index is among the lowest at 106.6 (national average base of 100), compared to 115.4 for Los Angeles, 116.8 for San Jose, 118.9 for San Diego, and 132.7 for San Francisco. In addition, Eastside tax rates rank below those of Seattle; in 1988 Bellevue's was at $11.10 per $1,000 valuation, compared to Seattle's $13.43.

What also makes the Eastside attractive are such things as sign codes, which don't allow the billboards that dominate the view in so many areas; hospitals that

Left: This attractive residential neighborhood can be found in Issaquah on East Lake Sammamish. Photo by Gary Greene

Below: Bellevue Square has played a pivotal role in the emergence of downtown Bellevue as a model for redevelopment. Photo by Gary Greene

are visionary in their approach to medicine; and schools where state and national recognition come yearly. When Bellevue Community College was seeking a new president in 1989, 177 applied for the job, which not only suggests how highly esteemed the college is, but speaks highly for the community as well.

Eastside communities offer an abundance of living opportunities. If there's a norm, it's a late-model house on a quiet, wooded lot in Bellevue, Redmond, or Woodinville. But what's a norm in an area with such diversity? Condos dominate along Lake Washington in Kirkland, drawing a young, active set that, on summer days, gives the place a Newport Beach, California, feel. In Woodinville's Hollywood Hills area, horses, trees, and open space are the drawing cards.

At the 1988 "Street of Dreams," on a hill outside Issaquah, new houses were selling in the $500,000 range. In Bothell, buyers will find plenty of houses in the more affordable five-figure range. Along the "Gold Coast" area of Medina, stately, older houses are found, a Mercedes or two in the circular driveways. When Hollywood needed a plush house to film a scene from the television movie, "Jacqueline Bouvier Kennedy," it didn't choose Beverly Hills. It chose Medina. On the opposite side of the Eastside, the fields are dotted with turn-of-the-century farmhouses.

In downtown Bellevue the 17-story Pacific Regent, built in 1987, offers plush living for senior citizens, living that includes Halloween parties and trips to Hawaii. And, on the Sammamish Plateau, a master-planned community, Klahanie, has proven to be the hottest-selling development on the Eastside, particularly for young families. Complete with tennis courts, a lake, and a stringent community code, Klahanie is expected to have 8,000 residents by the year 2000.

Striking scenery, quality schools, a low crime rate, and a strong economy make the Eastside a first choice for those interested in raising a family. Photo by Eric Draper

The Key to Quality: People

The Eastside didn't happen by accident. It was created by people. People with a vision. "The resource that's often overlooked in developing a first-class community is leadership," said Jim Hebert, president of Hebert Research Inc. "People here are community- and service-oriented. They have their priorities right."

Kemper Freeman echoes Hebert's thoughts. He refers to "they"—that almost invisible group of people who help make a place special. They are the ones who take the risks, join the planning commissions, voice their opinions at city hall. "Bellevue and the Eastside seem to have a high percent of 'theys,'" Freeman said. "And it's just not your people in politics and business. It's folks who care, period."

In Bellevue the first phase of the new downtown park—$1.8 million worth—was paid for by private funds. In Kirkland a new "Plaza of Champions" has been built to honor citizens who have brought wide recognition to themselves and the city. When King County threatened to ground hot-air balloons in the Sammamish Valley for liability reasons, citizens banded together and convinced officials to compromise. In a 1987 poll, Hebert Research asked Eastsiders to assess their community pride on a 1-to-10 basis, 10 being highest. The average response was 7.89.

Eastside city council meetings tend to be spirited, but spirit makes a city work, according to a *Journal American* reporter who had recently transplanted herself from Florida. "I can remember elections [in Florida] for city council in which just nine percent of the registered voters cast ballots," wrote Katherine Long in a 1989 opinion piece. Controversy, something she seldom saw in Florida, ultimately leads to better communities, Long wrote, because it shows people care. "I believe I'm in the company of people who care very deeply about the quality of their community and their environment," she wrote.

So who are these people? At last count some 74 people included in *Who's Who in America* lived on the Eastside. Generally, Eastsiders are well educated and have above-average incomes. Republicans outnumber Democrats two to one. But, as the *Seattle Times' Pacific Magazine* pointed out, "scratch Bellevue and up will pop an interesting crop of 'for instances' that belie the upper-middle-class white suburban stereotype." The magazine pointed out that the Eastside has a growing diversity. Eighteen percent of students in the Bellevue School District in 1988-1989 were minority students. In addition, while no shortage of wealth exists, there is a growing number of "working poor," and nearly one-third of Eastsiders are considered lower-middle or lower income, according to the Puget Sound Council of Governments.

Most Eastsiders are from somewhere else; only 13 percent were born here. But regardless of their backgrounds, all call the Eastside home. Together they form the fabric of a region that, over the last century, has grown from an isolated afterthought to a place that has it all—cities and suburbs, work and play, high tech and low taxes—in many respects, the best of all worlds.

A local audience relaxes to the smooth sounds that fill the air during the Bellevue Jazz Festival. Photo by Eric Draper

2 LOOKING BACK

I t was looked upon by many land seekers as an area not worth taming: thick with trees and wild blackberries, nearly void of trails, and separated from the local population center, Seattle, by a lake that was more than three miles wide in places—enough to test the callouses of even the most ardent oarsmen. But the land that comprises Bellevue today intrigued a few folks back in the nineteenth century. One of them was William Meydenbauer.

In March 1869 the German-born Meydenbauer rowed from his home at Leschi Park on Lake Washington's western shore to the bay on the eastern shore that is now adjacent to downtown Bellevue. There, he laid claim to a 40-acre piece of land and built a cabin. Meydenbauer was not your typical frontiersman; he was a baker. And he was not looking to roll up his sleeves and create a new town; he was looking for a weekend and summer getaway. But whatever his makeup and whatever his motive, Meydenbauer became the first person to establish a land claim in what is now Bellevue.

Now a bustling community with a booming economy, the Bellevue of 120 years ago was neither. At that time, Seattle itself had only 1,107 people. Only one other person, a Mr. McGilvra, lived on

Once considered not worth taming, the fertile landscape of the Eastside is now home to thousands. Photo by Eric Draper

the Seattle side of Lake Washington. Only Meydenbauer had a place on the Bellevue side. It was so quiet, Meydenbauer said, that while standing near his cabin in Bellevue he could hear McGilvra's dog barking across the lake.

For thousands of years only Indians had lived in the area, fished the lakes and streams, and hunted the abundant wildlife. But like most other Puget Sound Indians, they were ultimately victims of the white man's disease—small pox, in the 1830s—and government. Those who survived the epidemic were removed to reservations in the 1850s. Their Eastside heritage is preserved today in the naming of everything from Lake Sammamish to Tyee Grade School in Bellevue.

After Meydenbauer's initial claim, newcomers trickled into Bellevue, most having uprooted themselves from the Midwest and East. Among them were Aaron Mercer, whose brothers, Tom and Asa, had played big roles in Seattle's early history after coming west from Ohio; Clark M. Sturtevant, a Civil War veteran who took advantage of the law granting former soldiers 160 free acres, settling near what is now "auto row"; and John Zwiefelhofer, an Austrian cabinetmaker who came to the U.S. in 1860 and in 1879 settled where the Safeway Distribution Center is now located.

Growth was slow. This, remember, was an area that lived in the shadow of the city across Lake Washington, an area that lacked fertile prairie lands, an area that was not strategically located for transportation. No bridges connected it to Seattle. No major rivers rolled by. No railroads intersected it. In fact, roads in the 1870s did not pass through Bellevue but went around it, largely because of the bogs and other wetlands.

Still, settlers came. In 1882 Bellevue's first post office was established by Isaac Bechtel. Unnamed at the time, the town became Bellevue, although it isn't clear as to just how. It has been suggested that new settlers named it after another Bellevue in the Midwest, perhaps Bellevue, Ohio. Or that it was named because, in French, Bellevue means "beautiful view." At any rate, the town slowly emerging from the Eastside's towering firs at least had a name—and, though many didn't realize it at the time, quite a future.

A newspaper article in 1893 described the country as "a mine of wealth" needing only a good way to get its goods to market. The area had found its niche in supplying produce, particularly strawberries, to the Seattle market. But the fastest way to market was by ferry.

Besides produce, lumber was developing as a key industry in the late nineteenth century. Small logging camps dotted the area. The largest mill, at Wilburton, began operation in 1895. By the turn of the century, Wilburton had become something of a boomtown, with a population of 400.

Piece by piece, Bellevue grew into more than just a smattering of cabins and chicken coops. In 1903 the First Congressional Church was built. The church, since rebuilt, stands at the same location in downtown Bellevue today. In 1904 a north-south branch of the Northern Pacific Railroad bisected the Eastside, prompting construction of the Wilburton Trestle, said to be the tallest trestle in the world at the time. The Medina Grocery, one of the Eastside's oldest existing businesses, began operation in 1908, as did the Bellevue Mercantile Company.

Still, an item in a 1909 *Medina Booster* newspaper suggested that the area was still relatively sleepy. "The editors," said the paper, "do not think it necessary to print the boat schedule in the paper [because] . . . any time a person wants to go to Seattle, all they have to do is sit on the dock and whistle and the boat will come for them."

The area gradually changed. Electricity arrived in 1913, telephones three years later. With much of Bellevue's timber having been cut, the lumber industry slowed; Wilburton shut its mill in 1918.

In the same year, the American Pacific Whaling Company, which hunted whales in Alaska, chose Meydenbauer Bay to winter its fleet of seven vessels. It added some color and prestige to Bellevue, as did the Lake Washington Strawberry Festival. Begun in 1918, the annual event drew thousands of people from Seattle each year for tastes of luscious strawberries, most of which were grown by Bellevue's Japanese farmers.

It was time, some Bellevueites decided, to get serious about developing their town. In 1919 the Bellevue District Business Men's Association was formed around a stove in a general store. The Bellevue Commercial Club debuted in 1920, and next came the Bellevue District Development Club.

In a 1920 brochure touting the town, Bellevue was described as "a thriving community that now has three stores, three grade schools, one high school, two churches, one blacksmith shop, one sawmill, one post office, no saloons and plenty of fresh air." But even though by 1922 it was possible to drive the entire distance around Lake Washington, Bellevue was still not a magnet for people who wanted to put down roots. From 1920 to 1930 the number of businesses in Bellevue grew from 10 to 50, but the population grew more modestly, from 2,500 to 3,000. Though it was making progress, Bellevue was still regarded mainly as a weekend and summer haven for Seattle's wealthy.

Which made people all the more skeptical when James S. Ditty, in 1928, started predicting big, big things for the Eastside. One of Bellevue's first developers, Ditty boldly predicted a day when the Eastside would be home to 200,000 persons. He pushed for the incorporation of Bellevue. He devised a detailed plan for a model Eastside, which included the bridging of Lake Washington and an area filled with airports and golf courses. Though Ditty, an avid golfer, had big ideas, his address was better than his follow-through; as he admitted himself, Ditty, like a lot of others, "sat on the fence waiting for Bellevue to grow up."

It took some time. In 1931 C.W. Bovee pushed for incorporation. "We have the unusual distinction of being the sloppiest looking main street on the Eastside," he said. But he didn't get much support. What Bellevue really needed, others said, was access to Seattle. Bluntly, it needed a bridge across Lake Washington.

The ferries were fine for Seattleites who had summer places on the Eastside. Even some permanent residents of the Eastside were content with commuting daily to Seattle for business. But if the area was ever going to shake its sluggish growth, it had to connect with Seattle.

A bridge had been discussed as early as 1926, but it wasn't until 1930 that the discussion got serious. That was largely because the man doing much of the talking was Miller Freeman, a man whose name would soon become synonymous with the evolution of Bellevue as a first-class city.

Freeman, father of Bellevue Square developer Kemper Freeman, Sr., and grandfather of Bellevue Place developer Kemper Freeman, Jr., had been a driving force behind the building of the Lake Washington Ship Canal in 1916. Owner of a Seattle publishing house and a string of industrial journals, he and his family had moved into a 14-room mansion on Medina's Groat Point in 1928.

Freeman, who held plenty of political clout, argued that since a good highway had been built across Snoqualmie Pass, the bridge would complete a market roadway from Eastern Washington to the tidewater of Seattle. Because the lake was so wide and deep, Homer M. Hadley, a Seattle structural engineer, proposed a floating bridge, a revival of the pontoon bridges used by Roman legions some 18 centuries earlier.

Some, particularly those in Seattle, scoffed at the idea. *Seattle Times* publisher Clarence B. Blethen said it was a gigantic folly and his paper ran cartoons showing broken chunks of concrete on a desolate shore as the only remains of the venture. But the *Post-Intelligencer* supported it. So, too, did the *Bellevue American.*

On July 4, 1940, the Lacey Murrow Bridge, commonly known as the Mercer Island Bridge, was dedicated, opening a world of potential for Eastside economic development. "Fifteen minutes to your home in the country," expounded a Bellevue real estate advertisement. A Bellevue-to-Seattle bus service started, offering 26 trips daily. And, perhaps just as satisfying to some Eastsiders, Blethen, the *Times* publisher, publicly ate crow, admitting the pontoon concept was a complete success.

Unlike some other places, Bellevue had not been devastated by the Great Depression in the preceding decade. There were no factories to close. There was no drought to curtail strawberry production. Many of its residents continued to live comfortably on what became known as the "Gold Coast" of Lake Washington. Thus, when the bridge opened, the Eastside's future looked sunny.

World War II clouded the picture for four years; particularly dark was the period after Pearl Harbor when Bellevue's 300 Japanese residents were forced by the U.S. government to leave for internment camps in California. But once the war ended in 1945, Bellevue's outlook was bright again. And much of that was because of Miller Freeman's son, Kemper Sr., who ushered in a Bellevue boom that is still in progress.

During the war Freeman operated a shipbuilding business for the government in Port Angeles. When the war ended he began planning a business that would become Bellevue's cornerstone: Bellevue Square shopping center. The development of the square changed the course of development on the Eastside. Renovated in 1981, Bellevue Square has become one of the nation's most successful shopping centers.

The original 16-business square, among the first suburban shopping centers in the country, gave Bellevue "a surge of life in the community," according to *Seattle Times* reporter Dorothy Bran in 1947. In the 1950s Bellevue's population soared 54 percent to 12,291 residents. The Bellevue Chamber of Commerce, which had been formed in 1946 as an outgrowth of the Bellevue District Business Men's Association, touted the town as the Eastside's hub, a title that had belonged to Kirkland until then.

As early as 1942 the Business Men's Association had emphatically pushed for Bellevue's incorporation. By 1950 the population had increased to 8,000 people, and with the growth in population came the need for upgraded roads, sewers, and water lines. After a failed attempt in 1951, town officials put the incorporation measure before voters again on March 24, 1953. This time the response was different. The proposal passed 885 to 461. Bellevue was officially a city.

For Bellevue, incorporation was yet another step toward the limelight for a place often cast in Seattle's shadow. Almost simultaneously, Bellevue got an economic shot in the arm when Safeway began building a major distribution center there. The project, said Freeman at the time, "marks a milestone in Bellevue's emergence as a modern, balanced community incorporating pleasant suburban living, convenient home service and suitable light industries properly located and providing local employment."

The first mayor, Charles W. Bovee—the same C.W. Bovee who had pushed for incorporation more than 20 years before—wasted little time turning Bellevue into the city many dreamed it could be. A planning commission was formed. A Central Business District was defined, as were zones for apartments and light industry. Bellevue Way was planned for six lanes, unheard of at that time. Utility districts were formed.

Only two years after it had been incorporated, the city whose first order of business was deciding whose house to hold the inaugural council meeting in was being honored as an All-American city. In 1955 the National Municipal League and *Look* magazine chose Bellevue for the honor over 137 other cities. "Your comprehensive plan for traffic diversion, a controlled business district and an industrial park has gained national recognition," said *Look* editor Pete Dailey. "You have grappled with phenomenal growth and won."

The city celebrated with a parade, a banquet, fireworks, and a ball, then went about the business of grappling with more phenomenal growth. When Puget Sound Power & Light erected a four-story, $2-million structure in downtown Bellevue in 1956, Freeman saw it as a sign of independence. "We are no longer a bedroom community for Seattle," he said. "We are a job center."

In publications, the Bellevue of the late 1950s was touted as a place for "gracious living," a place where developers built quality neighborhoods, not row homes, where planning was a priority, and where "everything was aimed at orderly growth." In 1961 alone, three major businesses opened: Crossroads Shopping Center, United Control Electronics, and American Wholesale Grocery's distribution center. Developer Bert McNae began selling land that would soon become the Overlake Park industrial district. Lake Hills, 1,200 acres of former dairy farm, was heralded as the first major planned community in the Northwest. Some 4,000 homes eventually would be built in the development, with prices ranging from $13,000 to $22,000 in 1958. Meanwhile, roads were built. Apartments sprang up. And in 1962, Overlake Hospital opened.

If the hospital gave a boost to the community's physical health, a project completed the following year boosted its economic health: the Evergreen Point Floating Bridge. Throughout the 1950s, people on both sides of the lake haggled over whether a second bridge should be built, where it should be built, and how it should be paid for. Seattle's business community was cool on the idea; businessmen there saw the bridge as funneling people and money away from Seattle.

"They hired public relations people to fight the bridge, and they used many shrewd tactics," editorialized the late Bruce Helberg, publisher of the *Bellevue American*, in 1963. "They painted horror pictures of a lake paved with bridges . . . But they were never able to split the Eastside communities into warring factions. As a result, the 'little people of the Eastside' pushed doggedly on in the face of overwhelming odds."

The so-called Wallace Plan finally got the financially plagued project off the ground. Scott Wallace, a King County commissioner from the Eastside, proposed

The Evergreen Point Floating Bridge is shown here during construction in March 1963. This view faces east toward Bellevue. Courtesy, Post-Intelligencer Collection/ Museum of History and Industry

that the county underwrite $12 million of the $34-million cost of the bridge. The proposal passed, the Washington Supreme Court upheld the financing process, and construction began.

When the bridge opened in August 1963, so did a new chapter in the growth of the Eastside, particularly in the suburbs to the east. In the two years after the bridge opened, Bellevue's population increased 34 percent to 18,900. By the mid-1960s, Bellevue property values were rising 9 to 15 percent per year.

Work had begun on Interstate 405, the Eastside's last major transportation link.

Bellevue took on a new air of prestige, becoming a place known not only for growth, but for well-rounded growth that included the areas of business, education, and leisure. Among the newcomers to Bellevue in the mid- to late-1960s were the city hall building (1964), Bellevue Community College (1966), Bellevue Municipal Golf Course (1967), Bellevue Public Library (1967), the Bellevue Philharmonic Orchestra (1967), and the 13-story Bellevue Business Center (1969).

Annexations and newcomers swelled the population to 61,196 by 1970, helping Bellevue surpass Everett as the state's fourth largest city. In light of what went on in the 1960s, the 1970s were relatively quiet. Among the decade's highlights were the opening of Sears (1971), the founding of *The Journal American* (1976), and Bellevue Square's successful campaign to halt development of the proposed Evergreen East shopping center to maintain its stronghold on the Eastside.

In 1982, when Kemper Freeman, Sr., died, it was, as *The Journal American* suggested, "the end of an era, the suburban era. In its place is an era of increasing urbanization for the Eastside, and particularly Bellevue." The city's downtown business ordinance, put in place in 1981, raised the height limitations on buildings, and the Central Business District flourished. In fact, on the day Freeman died, a new group of business leaders—office-building developers—were celebrating the topping out of the 21-story One Bellevue Center at 108th Avenue N.E. and N.E. 4th Street. In a sense, it was a symbolic changing of the guards, a reaching upward instead of outward.

The classy new tower of glass served as a reminder of how far Bellevue had come from that day when, more than a century before, at a spot not more than a mile from the new high rise, William Meydenbauer had first staked his claim on land that became the city of Bellevue.

Kirkland

Had Kirkland's founders had their way, the town would look much different than it does today. The focal point would be a steel mill, for Peter Kirk's dream was to make the city the Pittsburgh of the West.

The idea actually began with Leigh S.J. Hunt, owner of the *Seattle Post-*

Intelligencer and the man for whom Hunts Point was named. In the late 1880s, some 15 years after the McGregors and Frenches first homesteaded on the site of present-day Kirkland, Hunt proposed locating a steel mill just above Houghton. His partner was Kirk, a wealthy English industrialist who saw great potential in making steel rails for a world market.

The plan was to mine ore from the Cascades, 60 miles away, and ship it, by rail, to Kirkland for reduction to steel. With financial backing from Seattle and elsewhere, the two formed the Moss Bay Iron and Steel Works of America and the Kirkland Land and Improvement Company. They platted a townsite large enough for 50,000 people, calling it Kirkland in honor of the company's principal owner.

The new town flourished. Kirk built his brick headquarters on a site that's now the intersection of Market Street and Central Way. There was speculation that Kirkland might outgrow Seattle, which had been devastated by fire in 1889. The new community was known nationwide as a place teeming with promise. Three thousand people were expected to be employed.

But the dream died before the first shipment of ore could roll into town. Among the reasons: A promised railroad line from the mine site to Kirkland was slow in coming, and much of the high-quality coal found at the mine proved inaccessible. The death knell was sounded by the Panic of 1893, the nationwide economic downturn that prompted some of the project's investors to back out of the steel venture altogether. More than one million dollars was lost on the deal.

However, unlike other towns in similar situations, Kirkland didn't become a ghost town. Much of the economic slack was picked up by the town's woolen mill—the state's first—which had started operations in 1892. By 1915 it employed 100 people, and it doubled that number during World War I. But fires in 1924 and 1935, coupled with a declining market, put an end to the mill.

In the meantime, shipbuilding was growing on the Kirkland waterfront. The Curtis family had begun the business in 1901, just north of where the Carillon Point development now stands. Six years later it was purchased by John L. Anderson and it became the Lake Washington Shipyard. Business boomed during World War II, when at one point 6,000 people were employed building navy ships. By 1950, however, with the war over, the shipyard became idle.

A merger and an annexation have greatly increased Kirkland's population and size since the late 1960s, though it has remained a mostly residential city with small businesses. In 1968 Houghton merged with Kirkland, giving the city 13,500 people. And in 1988 the city annexed Rose Hill, increasing the area of Kirkland by 50 percent and the population by 75 percent to 35,823. In doing so, Kirkland jumped from the state's 23rd largest city to its 11th.

Redmond

In 1871, two years after William Meydenbauer staked a claim in what became Bellevue, Luke McRedmond, along with Warren W. Perrigo, settled in what is now the Sammamish Valley. McRedmond's original home stood on land that eventually became the Redmond Golf Course and is now planned as the site of the new Town Center shopping mall.

Known for some time as Salmonberg because of the abundance of dog salmon in the Sammamish River, the settlement officially became Redmond in honor of the

Irish-born pioneer who platted the townsite in 1891 and became the town's first mayor and postmaster.

In the beginning, logging was Redmond's major industry, meaning saloons did a brisk business and Saturday nights never lacked for revelry. But by the turn of the century, Redmond was also an important trading and transportation center, connected to the Snoqualmie Valley and Kirkland by a Western-style stagecoach, and to Seattle by steamers.

In 1912 Redmond was incorporated as a city. When the Sammamish Slough was originally straightened that same year, more farmland opened and the area soon became known for its excellent poultry, vegetable, and dairy products. Willowmoor Farm, operated by James W. Clise and his wife, Ann, produced world-class Ayrshire cattle and Morgan horses. The 420-acre farm was sold in 1928, and the land eventually was purchased by King County, which turned it into Marymoor Park. The two-story, 28-room "Clise Mansion" is now home of the Marymoor Museum.

Redmond grew slowly; its population in 1945 was 500 and in 1963 only 2,067. But like other Eastside communities, Redmond benefited greatly from the opening of the Evergreen Point Floating Bridge in 1963. With trips to Seattle more convenient, a number of companies moved to Redmond, including Sundstrand, Physio-Control, Eddie Bauer, Rocket Research, and Data I/O. From 1970 to 1980 Redmond was the fastest-growing city in the state, its population more than doubling to 23,318. The 1980s brought more of the same.

Issaquah

The Eastside's oldest incorporated town, Issaquah dates back to 1859, when coal was discovered by L.B. Andrews and David Mowrey. Among the earliest to claim land in the area was William Pickering, who had been appointed governor of the Washington Territory by Abraham Lincoln. He arrived in 1867. The area was known then as Squak, an Indian name of uncertain meaning. In 1888 the Seattle Lake Shore and Eastern Railroad made coal mining a profitable venture and the area grew. In 1892 Squak was incorporated and renamed Gilman, in honor of Daniel Hunt Gilman, a railroad officer and first owner of the coal company. When it was discovered that a town called Gilman already existed, the post office changed it to Olney. Finally, in 1899 it became Issaquah—and, thankfully, stayed that way.

As the coal industry grew, so did the agriculture and lumber industries. Dairy farms were particularly noteworthy in the area; the top farms belonged to the Andersons, Tibbets, and Pickerings. Most coal mining had died out by the 1920s, but by then the lumber industry was gaining strength. By the early 1920s, however, the present-day Somerset, Newport, and Horizon View areas had all been logged, and by the late 1930s most of the old-growth timber was gone. In 1935 the Issaquah Salmon Hatchery was built.

From 1888 to 1940 Issaquah's population varied from 500 to 1,000 people, but, buoyed by the new Lacey Murrow Bridge, it grew 50 percent from 1951 to 1961. The population of Issaquah and the surrounding area ballooned again in the 1980s as the Interstate 90 high-tech corridor expanded and residential development spread quickly across the Sammamish Plateau east of Lake Sammamish.

Bothell

In 1888 Civil War veteran David C. Bothell and his wife, Mary Ann, filed for the first plat of land in the community that now bears their name. The Bothells—they had seven children—operated a shingle and lumber mill. Squak Slough, later named the Sammamish River, was ideal for transporting logs into Lake Washington and then on to Seattle mills. New railroad lines increased sales potential for area lumber, helping open the region to further development.

In 1885, even before the Bothells' arrival, the riverboat *Squak* first steamed up Squak Slough, making it much easier for people to travel between the Bothell area and Seattle. In 1909, by a 79-70 margin, Bothell incorporated as a city. Although a disastrous fire hit the city two years later, by 1912 the Pacific Highway between Everett and Seattle was finished and Bothell became linked with the modern era of transportation and commerce.

In the 1980s Bothell's "backwoods" image was transformed completely, as The Technology Corridor sprang up along Interstate 405. By 1988 a downtown revitalization project was in the works.

Other Eastside Communities

Medina: Just north of where William Meydenbauer first claimed land, Medina got its start. In 1876 Thomas L. Dabney bought land on the point now named for him. One early arriver promoted "Flordeline" as a name for the community but it lost out to Medina, named in 1892 by Mrs. S.A. Belote for the Arabian holy city of Medina. The community was incorporated in 1955.

Hunts Point: Hunt, the *Seattle Post-Intelligencer* publisher, bought the narrow finger of land that he named after himself in the late nineteenth century. His reason for the purchase? He lived on Yarrow Point and wanted Hunts Point so he could cut down the tall evergreen trees which obstructed his view of Seattle. Eventually, Hunts Point became the permanent home for some of the Eastside's wealthiest residents, and became incorporated the same year Medina did.

Yarrow Point: Platted in 1901 and incorporated in 1959, this peninsula on Lake Washington once contained little other than summer homes for Seattle's wealthy. William Easter was the first to claim land there in 1886. He was followed shortly by Ole Hanks. Seattle businessmen Jacob Furth and Bailey Gatzert established summer homes there in the late 1880s, along with Hunt. Much of Yarrow Point was logged off in 1907 by Isaac Bechtel for a real estate firm that developed the area in subsequent years. It was named by early-day land developer R.D. McAusland for a line in the poem "Yarrow Revisited" by English poet William Wordsworth, which extolled the Yarrow River in County Selkirk, Scotland.

Clyde Hill: The town's name was coined by its first mayor as descriptive of its location on a hill bisected by 92nd Avenue N.E., which was known as Clyde Road until World War II. The road name was originally suggested by a Scotsman, who found the area reminiscent of the topography of the Firth of Clyde in his homeland. It was incorporated in 1953, the same year as Bellevue.

Beaux Arts: In 1908 this Lake Washington community was founded as an artistic colony patterned after the garden villages of England. Intended as an arts and crafts center of the Northwest, it settled for being a charming residential area, and was incorporated in 1954.

Juanita: An unincorporated area north of Kirkland, Juanita originally was known as Hubbard, after a logger who lived there. Mrs. Charles Terry renamed it Juanita. A sawmill started by Dorr Forbes in the 1880s shipped lumber and shingles across Lake Washington to Seattle. Juanita had its own ferry dock, served by the steamer *Urania* until 1916, when the lake's water level was lowered by the Lake Washington Ship Canal.

Newcastle: Located between Bellevue and Renton, the Newcastle-Coal Creek area once comprised a booming area built on profits from coal. The Lake Washington Coal Company shipped out 150 tons of coal in 1867. Some 600 buildings sprang up in the area, and, for a while, the settlement rivaled Seattle in population. But production gradually decreased as fuel oil began arriving from California's oil fields. Coal remained a major industry in the area until about 1920, though a few companies survived until after World War II. The area is now primarily suburban.

Woodinville: Ira and Susan Woodin claimed land in this area southeast of Bothell in 1872. Like most areas on the Eastside, it originally relied heavily on sawmills. The Seattle Lakeshore and Eastern Railroad arrived in 1877. Farming soon became important, and Fred Stimson's Hollywood Farm became known for its fine cattle and swine. The brick Hollywood schoolhouse still stands today, having been converted into shops. Woodinville remains unincorporated; a 1989 vote to become a city failed by just 14 votes.

Duvall: First called Cherry Valley, this community on the Snoqualmie River took shape in the 1870s. James Duvall, for whom the town was eventually named, was the first to claim land there in 1875. Duvall relocated in about 1909 to accommodate a railroad grade that the Great Northern Railway was completing. It was incorporated in 1913. Farming, particularly dairy farming, remains the economic anchor of this still-rural community.

Carnation: Another town on the Snoqualmie, Carnation has roots deep in the Indian culture. The area was once home to a sizable Snoqualmie Indian longhouse village and the Snoqualmie tribe's chief, Pat Kanim. Originally, the community was called "Tolt," an anglicized abbreviation of an Indian word meaning "swift running waters." It became Carnation in 1917, after the Carnation Stock Farms (now the Carnation Research Farms), which moved to the valley in 1910. It reverted back to Tolt in 1928, except for a few exceptions such as the post office, and finally became Carnation for good in 1951.

Fall City: Land claims were first filed here by James Taylor and the Boham Brothers, Edwin and George, in 1869. Located three miles below Snoqualmie Falls, Fall City built its first sawmill four years later. Several others followed. Steamboats began navigating the river as far as Fall City in the 1870s. Agriculture, dairy farming, railroads, and hydroelectric power later became important economic forces in unincorporated Fall City.

Snoqualmie Falls: Snoqualmie Falls, 268 feet high, had long been sacred to the area's Indians. Washington Territorial Governor William Pickering laid claim to 640 acres encompassing the falls in 1869, and his relatives later farmed it. In 1898 construction of the hydroelectric power station began, an astounding engineering feat for its time. The next year the Snoqualmie Falls Power Company was generating power for Tacoma and Seattle. A second plant was added below the falls in 1910, and enlarged in 1957.

Snoqualmie: In the 1860s the area around Snoqualmie was home to scattered pioneer families, most of whom were involved in farming, particularly in hops. In 1889 the Snoqualmie Land and Improvement Company platted the town, and it was incorporated in 1903.

North Bend: The gateway to King County from the east, North Bend sits below majestic Mount Si, named for Josiah "Uncle Si" Merritt, a pioneer who came to the valley in 1862. Matts Peterson first claimed land in the area in 1865. Agriculture, lumber, and coal were important to the region, as was its location on a route across Snoqualmie Pass, where a crude road had been built in 1865. Mary and Will Taylor platted the town in 1889, and it got its name from the northerly turn of the Snoqualmie River. It was incorporated in 1909.

Coal miners at the Newcastle mine pose for a group portrait. Courtesy, Bicentennial Collection, Renton Historical Society

3 BELLEVUE'S BURGEONING DOWNTOWN

A decade or so ago, two jokes about downtown Bellevue were making the rounds. The first joke about Bellevue's downtown was that there wasn't one. The second joke was that if there was one, it most certainly was the only downtown so dominated by parking lots that it was possible to traverse the area by car—without even using a street.

Now, following an extraordinary 10-year development period, nobody's laughing. They're applauding. They're applauding a downtown that has 11 buildings of at least 10 stories, more commercial space than the Portland central business district, and a park that *Sunset* magazine has called the city's "jewel in its crown." They're applauding a downtown whose driving force has been an uncommon blend of teamwork between the public and private sectors.

Significantly, the applause isn't just local chest-beating. Among the publications that have joined in are *Atlantic Monthly, Architecture, Sunset, USA Today*, and the *New York Times*.

"There isn't a city in the country with a more progressive urban design guideline than Bellevue," said William H. Whyte after touring Bellevue in 1985. And Whyte knows his stuff. He's perhaps the country's foremost authority on what makes downtown areas attractive or unattractive to people. The former editor of *Fortune* magazine, Whyte influenced New York City's planning code and

After 10 years of extraordinary development, Bellevue has 11 buildings of at least 10 stories and more commercial space than Portland.
Photo by Eric Draper

has written such books as *The Social Life of Small Urban Spaces, The Last Landscape,* and *The Organization Man.*

But beyond aesthetics, downtown Bellevue has admirable economic virtues. According to Dickwin Armstrong, president of the Bellevue Chamber of Commerce, in 1987 businesses moved into one million square feet of office space in Bellevue. The city *had* only one million square feet of total office space in 1980. As an employment base, downtown Bellevue grew some 38 percent in the 1980s, providing 30 percent of Bellevue's total jobs. Many Bellevue buildings now command higher rents than their counterparts in Seattle. And as a retail center, Bellevue's downtown, which represents only 15 percent of Bellevue's businesses, collected nearly one-third of the city's sales receipts in 1987.

What it all adds up to is a vibrant place—the hub of the Eastside economic wheel, second only to Seattle among other Washington downtowns in terms of commercial space. Those are lofty achievements for a downtown that, at the dawn of the 1980s, hardly existed.

Laying the Foundation

In recent years the blossoming of downtown Bellevue has been due to an uncommon marriage of the private and public sectors, the creative drive of both interests merging for a common goal: quality. But the framework for such quality was laid decades ago when Bellevue first became incorporated as a city.

"From the beginning, the planning commission never really looked at Bellevue as a small town," John F. Herman, a member the original commission, once told *The Journal American.* "These men had depth of vision." Take 104th Avenue, for example. In 1953 the idea of a six-lane street was ludicrous. But planners saw Bellevue's potential for growth, allowed for a six-lane street, and now six lanes are an absolute necessity.

Early on the planners envisioned a clearly defined business district (the Central Business District or CBD) bordering an equally defined residential district. "That's because the commission planned to avoid the blight area around the business district, as is so common in some cities," said Herman.

Such well-defined boundaries didn't always go over big with the public back in the early fifties; remember, zoning was something new for Bellevue. "Some persons regarded it as an invasion of personal rights," said Herman. "There were many hot fights over land uses. I'll never forget the night a lawyer took a swing at me during a meeting. Old-timers had no concept of the city that was to be. Many thought of it as a linear district stretching all the way to Kirkland along one main route, whereas we on the commission decided we wanted a compact core."

Though the borders were in place, city planners had difficulty making downtown a priority when the rest of Bellevue was booming with suburban growth in the 1960s and 1970s; city governments can only juggle so many balls. By the mid-1970s, however, it was time to deal with downtown. At the time, two separate skirmishes were being fought, both of which would play a key role in the emer-

Developers were encouraged to provide plazas and other public spaces with every project they undertook in an effort to create a balance between occupied and available land. Photo by Wolfgang Kaehler

45

gence of a new downtown.

One was the increasing amount of office and commercial development in Bellevue that had people cringing in some residential neighborhoods. "The city council and the community took a look at itself in the seventies and saw the danger of becoming Anyplace, U.S.A., with suburban sprawl, and said, 'We can't allow this to happen in Bellevue,'" said Caroline Robertson, president of the Bellevue Downtown Association (BDA). That led to a rezoning plan adopted in 1981 that concentrated new office, retail, and financial activities downtown to free residential neighborhoods from intense development pressure. The efforts of the BDA and the Bellevue Chamber of Commerce helped make the rezoning plan work.

The other catalyst, ironically, involved a tract of land some three miles away. It was called Evergreen East, a 120-acre parcel in what was then an unincorporated area between Redmond and Bellevue. And, in 1976, developer Edward J. DeBartolo of Youngstown, Ohio, had every intention of building a huge shopping mall on the site. Having built more than 125 shopping malls around the country, DeBartolo was a potent force and was used to getting his way.

His proposed shopping center gave Kemper Freeman, Sr., the impetus to devise a plan to double the size of Bellevue Square. Clearly, the Bellevue area wasn't big enough for two large shopping centers, and the strong-minded Freeman wasn't about to budge. If Evergreen were built, most figured, downtown would be doomed.

Downtown businesses, used to considering each other as the competition, realized Evergreen was now the competition and joined forces. City officials, meanwhile, realized how integral Bellevue Square was as downtown's retail core. Both forces united behind Freeman. In 1980 DeBartolo, after four years of political battles with Freeman, King County, and the City of Bellevue, dropped his plan to build the new mall. It was the first time he had ever failed to build a shopping center once one was announced. With DeBartolo's retreat, all eyes turned to Freeman and the redevelopment of Bellevue Square.

Bellevue Square

Among the descriptions of downtown Bellevue heard time and again is that it's unlike any downtown you've ever seen. Among the reasons is Bellevue Square, a 200-store shopping mall that sits on downtown's western edge. Few, if any, American cities have a shopping center in the heart of their downtown. And if anyone thought Kemper Freeman, Sr., was foolish to buck the odds and build it, they couldn't argue with the results. Bellevue Square has become one of the country's most successful shopping centers.

In 1987, 11.5 million people visited Bellevue Square, two-and-a-half times more than visited San Diego's Sea World. The store failure rate for malls in the U.S. is about 5 percent; Bellevue Square's is less than 1.5 percent. In King County the average shopper spends 41 minutes in a mall; at Bellevue Square nearly two hours. Total retail sales in 1987 were $957 million, accounting for more than one-third of all retail sales in Bellevue. The Square employs 3,000 people, including 600 at Nordstrom alone.

"It is definitely one of the Eastside's success stories," said James Hebert, whose Bellevue research firm keeps a steady finger on the area's economic pulse.

The 200-store Bellevue Square employs approximately 3,000 people and plays host to upwards of 11.5 million people each year. Photo by Gary Greene

As amazing as its success were the odds it beat to reach that success. In a sense, Bellevue Square broke all the rules, says Hebert. Rules, he said, such as never build a mall in an urban setting, always have nearby accessibility to a freeway, and never build a multilevel mall.

As they browse through the mall's diverse mix of stores, few shoppers probably realize what a gamble Bellevue Square was. The original Square, opened by Kemper Freeman, Sr., in 1946, was called "Freeman's Folly" by some doubters who wondered how a shopping center—a relatively new concept in 1946—expected to make a go of it in sleepy Bellevue. Freeman had never doubted his idea would work. Before breaking ground, he had driven to 22 shopping centers around the country seeking ideas and had borrowed money to the hilt. The original Square—16 stores—was so modest that its anchor tenant, Frederick & Nelson, wouldn't sign more than a two-year lease, and required Freeman to build the store.

Nordstrom was built in 1956, and by the 1970s it was apparent that expansion was needed. But the Freemans—Kemper Freeman, Jr., had joined his father's development business in the 1970s—faced more obstacles than just Evergreen East. Among the others: The Freemans had almost no experience as developers. The massive overhaul was going to cost $142 million. No public money was available. And prime lending rates had skyrocketed. But the Freemans, with the help of a team of experts they formed, beat the odds. Among other things, they secured a $34-million loan from Connecticut General, the largest shopping center loan the company had ever made. In 1981 the first phase of the redevelopment opened, and in 1984 the final phase was completed. Bellevue Square's size had nearly doubled to 900,000 square feet and it had four major tenants, with The Bon Marche and J.C. Penney joining Frederick & Nelson and Nordstrom.

"As a chamber of commerce professional, I've seen shopping malls all over the country," Dickwin Armstrong said, "but Bellevue Square *is* unique because it

Jungle Jim's at Bellevue Square offers weary pedestrians and shoppers a place to relax and eat. Photo by Gary Greene

doesn't overwhelm you with oversized storefronts and elongated lines. As you look down the mall, your eye is distracted by aspects of the architecture. Bellevue Square set the tone of quality for this city. It said 'If you do it in Bellevue, you've got to do it better.'"

The two-story, fully enclosed retail center is a considerable cut above the standard mall. Storefronts exude a sense of originality. Skylights bring in natural light. A cushioned boat attracts small children, who run, jump, and roll over it with endless energy. At center court the area beneath a giant clock has become Bellevue's quintessential meeting place. Nearby, a glass elevator quietly slides up and down, taking people to the second level for shopping or the third level for an afternoon at the Bellevue Art Museum, which pays one dollar a year in rent. Decked parking flanks the mall's western side, complete with valet service.

Such amenities, combined with a superb mix of stores, draw 30,000 to 40,000 shoppers per day, and 60,000 to 70,000 during the Christmas season. In 1988 the Square's sales were $350 per square foot, the highest volume for any large shopping center on the West Coast and more than double the industry average of $160. In a sense, the Square set the tempo for other businesses to come to downtown Bellevue. "It was a catalyst," said Robertson, the BDA president. "It gave downtown a success feeling."

Reaching for the Sky

As Bellevue Square was working on its redevelopment, Bellevue's City Council was finalizing a rezoning plan that would essentially revolutionize downtown. The plan, which went into effect in 1981 after years of refining, allowed downtown buildings to be taller—300 feet, or about 25 stories—and closer together. Though Bellevue already had two medium-rise buildings, the code ushered in a new era of "upward mobility." Suddenly, Seattleites looking across Lake Washington were seeing much more than trees and the Cascades.

After the rezoning, property values soared to $40-$60 a square foot from $6-$10 a square foot. In 1983 three new high rises were completed: the 24-story Skyline Tower (now CityFed Skyline Tower), the 21-story One Bellevue Center, and the 16-story Plaza Center. In 1986 the trio was joined by what are now Bellevue's two tallest buildings—the 27-story Koll Center Bellevue and the 25-story Security Pacific Plaza. The Pacific Regent, a 17-story retirement high rise, was completed in 1987. And in 1989 it was announced that Wright Runstad & Co. planned to build a 30-story, $70-million skyscraper in 1990 and 1991 that would be Bellevue's tallest.

The first phase of the CBD's most ambitious high-rise undertaking, Bellevue Place, opened in late 1988. The $150-million project, a mixed-use development headed by Kemper Freeman, Jr., includes the 24-story Hyatt Regency Hotel, the 21-story Seafirst Bank Tower, a 6-story office/retail building, and a 7-story glass-domed winter garden. The complex was expected to add 2,000 new jobs to the community and bring $25 million a year in tax receipts to city coffers.

Bellevue Square's success had already given downtown a strong retail core. The high rises were the perfect complement. "But what really gave downtown Bellevue credibility was when business owners in Seatttle said, 'My gosh, we need to have an office in Bellevue,'" said the BDA's Robertson.

Some CEOs weren't easily convinced, though. Freeman recalls a major Seattle firm that was doing an abundance of business on the Eastside in the early 1980s. Most of the staff lived on the Eastside, so each day they made a double commute—in the morning to Seattle to pick up papers and take them to Bellevue

The CityFed Skyline Tower stands 24 stories in downtown Bellevue. Photo by Gary Greene

for discussions with clients, then back again in the afternoon for office work. The staffers tried to convince the senior people that the company needed a Bellevue office. They were met with blank stares. "Why would we want to do that?" the senior staffers would say.

"Finally, after five years of debate, they loaded the leaders in a car and drove them here," said Freeman. "The leaders looked around and were amazed. They had no idea what Bellevue had become." Indeed, for businesspeople who stuck close to their Seattle offices, seeing Bellevue's new downtown was like an uncle rediscovering a seldom-seen niece—that cute little girl who had blossomed into a beautiful woman, seemingly overnight.

As companies set up shop in Bellevue, the influx created a "critical mass" of business. In the early 1980s the newcomers were primarily branch offices of Seattle businesses. But the second wave was big-league stuff: Seafirst Bank's corporate banking division, Big Eight accounting firms such as KPMG Peat Marwick and Touche Ross, law firms such as Bogle and Gates, and headquarters for such corporations as CityFed Mortgage, one of the largest mortgage banks in the country.

The result? By mid-1987 Bellevue had 7.5 million square feet of commercial

Koll Center Bellevue, the city's tallest building, stands 27 stories. It was completed in 1986. Photo by Wolfgang Kaehler

space. By comparison, Spokane and Tacoma, the second and third largest cities in the state, each had about 4 million. The Seafirst Building at Bellevue Place and the nine-story Quadrant Building on the eastern edge of the CBD added nearly 500,000 square feet to that total in 1988.

Symbolic of Bellevue's rise to prominence was the establishment, in 1988, of The Lakes Club atop the Security Pacific Plaza. The club, replete with $300,000 worth of cherry woodwork and $50,000 worth of Northwest art, is operated by Club Corporation of America, which manages more than 200 clubs in the U.S. and the Far East. It was, in a sense, the frosting on downtown's cake, giving the city another dash of prestige.

"Suburban centers, or 'urban villages' like Bellevue are nothing new," said Tom Bernard, a Bellevue developer and former chairman of the Bellevue Chamber of Commerce. "You see them around Boston, San Francisco, and Orange County. What is new is that Bellevue has taken a dramatically different and further step than most of those other areas. It's taken that step from the five-story Class-A downtown office buildings and become a true high-rise urban center."

How far has downtown Bellevue come in a decade? The same downtown that employed some 13,000 people in 1980 is expected to employ nearly double that by 1990.

Downtown as a People Place

At the same time Bellevue lifted the lid on downtown's height regulations, it also incorporated tight guidelines to make downtown "user friendly" from the street level. Toward that end, the city provided incentives for developers. For each amenity their building included—plazas, fountains, sculptures, attractive walls, and maximum retail frontages— developers were allowed to exceed, by some degree, the 300-foot limit.

"The city has set high standards," said Mark Hinshaw, the city's principal urban designer. "Without them you might get one nice building with a junky building next door."

Not surprisingly, city planners and private developers have clashed from time to time; the BDA's Robertson calls it "creative tension." But, generally, the relationship works. In fact, Bellevue's development has been considered something of a model because of its unusual blend of public and private interests. As *The Journal American* reported in 1986: "Some cities have great public involvement, or great private involvement, but few have both. Bellevue is one of them."

At the core of downtown's quality has been an attention to detail. When The Bon Marche was added to Bellevue Square in 1984, the city strongly encour-

The second tallest building in the Bellevue skyline, the 25-story Security Pacific Plaza was ready for occupancy in 1986. Photo by Gary Greene

aged the store to run a center aisle through its store, meaning people heading west on the pedestrian corridor could walk into the mall and to the Square's center court without obstructions. It might have seemed like a minor detail, but Hinshaw believes such decisions make the difference between a run-of-the-mill downtown and a first-class downtown. "Little things make a lot of difference," said Hinshaw, who studied under William H. Whyte.

For example, when the Security Pacific Plaza was planned, the blueprints called for a blank granite wall along 108th Avenue N.E. The city intervened, encouraging the architect to add something that would appeal to pedestrians. What came of that was a series of historic Bellevue vignettes etched in the granite. Likewise, when the Koll Center was being completed, architects came to the city with a design change; they had to put in two large exhaust vents from the parking garage just north of the building. Not acceptable, said the city, figure out something bet-

The Bon Marche was added to Bellevue Square in 1984 and incorporates a convenient center aisle which makes shopping easier. Photo by Gary Greene

ter. Weeks later, the developers came back with an idea for hiding the vents with circular sculptures featuring salmon and masking the vents' sound with waterfalls. Rather than detracting from downtown, the sculptures ultimately added a touch of class—and a Northwest feel—to it.

"A good example of meeting design challenges in Bellevue is the plan for the convention center to be located downtown," said Dickwin Armstrong. "The architects must design the center so that all sides, including the roof, will be visually appealing, because the center will be viewed by the public from all sides. Building details like that make Bellevue's look a special one."

But if city planners deserve credit for Bellevue's emerging downtown, so do developers. Consider the lengths Wright Runstad & Co. went to in building and landscaping the successful Security Pacific Plaza. The focal point of the lobby is an artistic archway whose blocks of stone were shipped from Spain to Italy, where they were cut and carved. The stone for the lobby floor came from South Dakota and Canada. Outside, some trees and shrubs were handpicked by a Wright Runstad representative at a New Jersey nursery.

Whyte, the urban design expert who writes extensively of Bellevue in his book, *City: Rediscovering the Center,* has praised the city for the "noble undertaking" of designing a new downtown with the pedestrian in mind. He said Bellevue is one of only about four cities in the country whose zoning recognizes that "the street is the river of life in a city." He has been impressed with everything from the overall look of downtown—it has, he says, "a nice, compact look that sort of says, 'This is a city'" —to the movable chairs at Bellevue Square's center court, which allow people control over the environment.

Whyte isn't the only one heralding Bellevue's downtown. In 1988 Don Canty, editor of *Architecture* magazine, selected Bellevue, Baltimore, and Charleston, South Carolina, as up-and-coming U.S. cities with the most progressive architectural designs. Later that year *Architectural Digest* writer Douglas Gantenbein wrote: "[Bellevue] has everything an urban planner could hope for—economic vitality, a strong sense of community, consistent political leadership—and its citizens seem genuinely proud of their city."

A Park is Born

Another example of the hand-in-hand spirit of Bellevue's private and public sectors is the new downtown park. Located on a 17.5-acre parcel just south of Bellevue Square, it opened in the fall of 1987. Its first phase, the 7.5-acre eastern section, included gardens, trees, a canal, a waterfall, and a promenade that formed a ring around a large meadow of grass. It is a "passive," not an "active," park, meaning it was designed more as a place to come and relax than, say, play softball.

But as intriguing as the European-flavored park itself is the way it came about. It was a cooperative effort between the city and a private group, the Bellevue Downtown Park Citizens Committee. An international competition was held to design the park. Meanwhile, after a public bond issue failed, the citizens group raised $1.8 million in corporate and private donations to fund the first phase. In a most uncommon procedure, the city council approved a one-dollar-per-year lease to the private group. Once the first phase was completed, the park was turned over to the city. In September 1988 voters approved a $16.5-million park bond issue, $3 million of which will go to completing the second phase of the park.

Sunset magazine said in 1988 that Bellevue's new park symbolizes that the community is coming to grips with its evolution from a suburb of Seattle to the state's fourth largest city. "The new park offers a graphic example of a community redefining itself in urban terms," wrote *Sunset*'s Daniel Gregory and Peter Fish. They said the park helps "give Bellevue a strongly focused, easily identifiable center." The magazine chose downtown Bellevue for its story on "Can the West Grow Wisely?" because, Gregory told *The Journal American*, "it seemed to be the best example of a city looking to its future and designing for its future."

Like most burgeoning cities, Bellevue has faced the challenge of increased traffic. But rather than cross their fingers and hope the problem would magically vanish, citizens, city officials, and business representatives have resolved to confront it. In 1988 two groups were formed to do just that. The Traffic Impact Task Force began concentrating on a proposal for managing new development and apportioning the cost of traffic improvements. The

Bellevue has approached the problem of traffic with proven foresight. This is reflected in the size of local streets and highways. Photo by Eric Draper

Facing page: Bellevue's new skyline has been one positive indicator of the growth the region has experienced. Photo by Wolfgang Kaehler

Below: Bellevue's downtown park, called the city's "jewel in its crown" by Sunset *magazine, included, in its first phase development, gardens, trees, a canal, a waterfall, and a promenade that formed a ring around a large meadow of grass. Photo by Gary Greene*

Bellevue Alliance for Transportation Solutions was formed as a broad-based group to seek and promote solutions for traffic problems.

Prior to either group's existence, the Transportation Management Association (TMA) was already in action, promoting ride-sharing and the use of Metro buses and van pools to downtown Bellevue. The TMA has gained national attention because of its uncommon makeup; it is a partnership of the city, the BDA, and Metro. Most of the nation's transportation services are provided by a private body or a public body, but not by both.

Because of such forward thinking, Bellevue's downtown continues to draw national attention. Among its fans is Neal R. Peirce, a nationally syndicated newspaper columnist who specializes on urban issues. He has been impressed with Bellevue's metamorphosis from a typical suburban city to a what he calls a "Class-A municipality."

Bellevue's transition has been fueled, he says, by people with vision. "This intrepid bunch believes it's possible to create a 'there there'—to influence building materials, the shape of new buildings, the flow of traffic and pedestrians—to create a distinguished city even when there's little established urban form or context to relate to. It's an audacious idea; to my knowledge, it's never occurred anywhere else. But if it works, it will be a landmark."

4
HIGH TIMES FOR HIGH TECH

As the Eastside's architectural anchor, Bellevue's downtown symbolizes the city's rise to prominence among midsized U.S. cities. But even though downtown may be the most visible sign of progress in Bellevue and across the Eastside, it does not stand alone in the spotlight. Instead, it is joined by a cast of companies that is quietly turning the Eastside into one of the country's hotbeds of high tech. Beyond downtown Bellevue are corporations that produce everything from software for NASA to video games for children to the "black box" flight recorders for airplanes.

"As in the Silicon Valley itself three decades ago, a raw excitement is building [in Bellevue]," said Portland-based *Northwest* magazine as the high-tech boom swelled in 1985. "A kind of Old West feeling pervades the place. A sense of being at the edge of a barefisted frontier where fortunes exist for the taking . . ."

That frontier has opened up on Interstate 90 to the east, Interstate 405 to the north, and numerous pockets in between. Redmond, Bothell, Bellevue, Kirkland, and Issaquah—all the major Eastside cities are home to this thriving industry that only a decade ago hardly existed here.

Most of the Eastside's high-tech companies make software, the programming that directs computers. But in this field, diversity runs deep. Some specialize in medical equipment or biotechnology, others in electronics or aerospace devices. All are playing a role in bolstering the Eastside economy and attracting national attention in the process. *American Demographics,* a consumer-markets magazine based in New York, lists Washington in a select group of high-tech trailblazers that includes only California, New England, and New Jersey. The Association of Biotech Companies lists the Puget Sound area as one of its top five areas in the country.

Even without Boeing, high tech is bigger in Washington than the state's lumber industry. And applause for the state or Puget Sound must be amplified for the Eastside itself, because in

High tech on the Eastside, encompassing everything from software to health care, has enjoyed tremendous success in recent years. Courtesy, TSW/Click-Chicago, Ltd.

Washington, the Eastside is the heart of high tech. Although the area has only 7 percent of the state's population, it is home to 35 percent of the state's high-tech companies, according to the "Advanced Technology in Washington State 1989 Directory." More than 405 high-tech firms have sunk roots on the Eastside. Bellevue leads the way with 178, followed by Redmond with 100, Bothell with 50, Kirkland with 46, Woodinville with 18, and Issaquah with 11.

Just how hot is high tech on the Eastside? In 1988 the American Electronics Association reported that the state's high-tech industry makes goods worth $2.7 billion. The Eastside accounts for about 58 percent of that $2.7 billion.

High-Tech Employment

When *The Journal American* commissioned a survey in 1988 to determine how Eastsiders were employed, it found this: Whereas the majority of Eastsiders once worked in Seattle, fewer than one-fourth do now. Meanwhile, nearly 40 percent—52,500—work directly, or indirectly, for Eastside high-tech firms.

As important as high tech's direct effect on the economy is, the spin-off business it creates is equally important. One job in four on the Eastside owes its existence, directly or indirectly, to high tech, according to the survey. For every Eastsider who works directly for a high-tech company, two have jobs made possible by that company. "The [high-tech] industry feeds a lot of companies," said Robert Fulton, chairman of the Washington Software Board and president of Generic

*Koll Business Center in
Bothell stands along the
Interstate 405 "Technology
Corridor." Photo by Gary
Greene*

Software. "There are printing documentation and accounting firms, for example. Practically every major law firm on the Eastside the last two years has brought on one or more specialists in software."

Growth in the Eastside's high-tech industry will add more than 100,000 new jobs to the local economy by the year 1992, according to *The J-A.* That would mean a phenomenal 58 percent increase. Wrote a *J-A* editorialist: ". . . the change underscores the continuing evolution of the Eastside as a distinct community—no longer just a place where 'Seattleites' sleep . . . If regional growth trends were patterned the same way television series are propagated, then the Eastside would be well on its way to success as a spinoff."

Further pointing to the Eastside's vibrant economy is an unemployment rate that traditionally is one to two percentage points lower than the Seattle area. Employment, not unemployment, makes news on the Eastside. Leading the way as the Eastside's largest high-tech employers are Redmond-based Microsoft, which started with two employees in 1975 and now has some 3,000; Boeing Computer Services, with 2,500 of its 11,000 employees working in Bellevue; Redmond-based Sundstrand Data Control (1,534); Redmond-based Physio-Control (800); and Bothell-based Advanced Technology Laboratories (700).

In terms of sales, the Eastside's top high-tech firms in 1988 were Boeing Computer Services, Nintendo of America in Redmond, Microsoft Corp., Sundstrand, Advanced Technology Laboratories (ATL), Spacelabs in Redmond, Physio-Control, Data I/O in Redmond, and Olin's Defense Systems in Redmond.

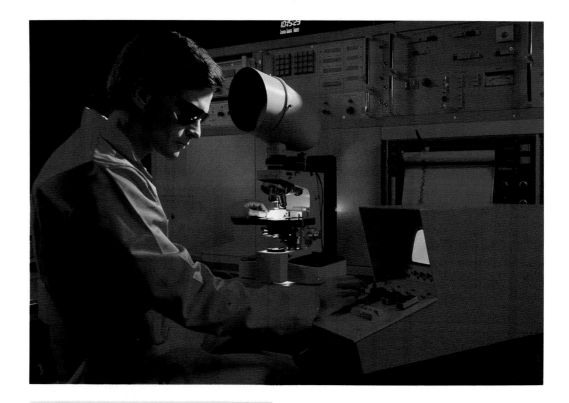

The Roots of Eastside High Tech

In the beginning was Boeing. Though for statistical purposes most don't consider the engineering endeavors of the aerospace company as "high tech," most agree it triggered the early high-tech companies. If Boeing is considered the father of the local industry, then Redmond-based United Control Corporation (which merged with Sundstrand in 1967) must be considered the mother. The following is a condensed look at how the high-tech family grew, based on a flowchart designed in 1978 by four ex-Boeing employees: Bob Hancock, Orlien Brecker, Hy Pollack, and Bruno Strauss.

In 1961 United Control moved to Redmond, one of a handful of companies that quietly grew until the first small high-tech boom in the late 1960s. It was then that several of United Control's employees struck out on their own. Phil Linwick started Integrated Circuits Inc. in Redmond. Ralph Astengo founded Advanced Technology Laboratories in Bellevue. Jerry Paros founded Paroscientific Inc. in Redmond. Meanwhile, Milton Zeutschel and Grant Record left Automix Keyboards Inc. and founded Data I/O in Redmond. Leo Pratt moved Pacific Electro Dynamics to Bellevue. And Don Jenkins left John Fluke Manufacturing to found the Universal Manufacturing Company Inc. in Woodinville.

The boom was on, fueled by the 1969 Boeing bust, which left 20,000 employees out of work and many of them eager to start something new. In the early 1970s Boeing itself joined the high-tech race, creating Boeing Computer Services. Throughout the seventies, countless firms branched off from companies that were still in infancy themselves. Physio-Control moved to the Eastside in 1974. Then came Microsoft in 1975, adding software to the mix of high-tech ventures. Though the name of Bill Gates' company would soon be uttered worldwide, it alone was not responsible for the area's software boom.

"The fact is that before Gates ever graduated from grade school, the Puget Sound region had a high-tech infrastructure solidly in place," said *Northwest* magazine in 1985. "It was this infrastructure, as much as it was the historical accident that Gates had been raised in Seattle, that was to allow Bellevue to accelerate from bedroom community to Bauhaus in less than a decade's time."

The software explosion started about 1980. Microrim was born from Boeing Computer Services in 1981. Microsoft, meanwhile, has brought forth a growing list of companies that includes Midisoft, Computer Product Introductions, Renaissance GRX, Asymetrix, Info Express, and Raima Corp. In 1983 the Eastside surpassed Seattle in number of high-tech companies. For spin-off firms the Eastside was simply the logical place to locate; a high-tech network was already in place and skilled employees were available.

As the 1980s progressed, however, more out-of-state companies chose the Eastside, too. Among them was Bright Star Technology Inc., whose new "HyperAnimation" technology allows a lifelike image on an Apple Macintosh computer to talk. (The technology was featured in a 1988 Walt Disney TV version of the movie, *The Absent-Minded Professor*.) In the mid-1980s, as Elon Gasper of California refined the new technology, he carefully considered where to anchor his new company. Ultimately, he chose Bellevue, where the company started in 1987. "I picked the Eastside because it's a very dynamic area," he told *The Journal American*. "There are a

Though the region now includes more than 150 successful high-tech firms, Boeing remains a potent force and a significant Eastside employer. Courtesy, TSW/Click-Chicago, Ltd.

number of new companies that are all working in synergy. There is a critical mass of well-known companies here. You have Microsoft, Aldus, Microrim and, of course, Boeing. It's also very nice to live here. And for the future this is a good place to grow a company."

Software Sets the Pace

At the core of the Eastside's high-tech industry is software. In 1988 some 450 software companies, employing some 7,000 people, were doing business in Washington, the bulk of them on the Eastside. In the four-year period from 1984 to 1988, the state's software industry quadrupled to sales of $1.5 billion. By 1988 the industry was already three times as large as the state's apple industry, which is the nation's leader. The state's software companies now produce roughly one-third of the country's software for microcomputers, making Washington the third largest producer of PC software.

"It's mostly an exporting industry, to other states and to other countries," said Chang Mook Sohn, Washington State chief economist. This export-oriented industry draws more outside money into the state. At the same time, the industry typically pays higher wages, from which the region profits even more.

Two reasons why this area has become such a software hotbed are Redmond-based Microsoft, the world's leading independent software developer, and Issaquah-based Egghead Software, the nation's largest software retailer. "Egghead is driving the market from the retail end and Microsoft from the development end," said Fulton.

For Eastside software companies, it's the best of both worlds. "Microsoft is in a key position in that it dominates the operating systems," said Fulton. "It's more powerful than IBM. So it's an advantage to be here [as a software company] as opposed to being in, say, Cleveland. You can drive over to have lunch with someone from Microsoft."

Likewise, being in Egghead's backyard gives software companies a better crack at having their product make the company's much-coveted shelves, says Fulton. In addition, the concentration of software companies opens up all sorts of possibilities for growth. "In the software business, there's lots of codevelopment," said Fulton. For example, Fulton's company, Generic Software, sometimes works with a handful of other companies on a project. "We exchange technology," he said. "We just had a company move down here from Anchorage. They wanted to be where the action is."

And the Eastside definitely is where the action is. Based on 1987 revenues, 18 of Puget Sound's top 25 software manufacturers were located on the Eastside, according to the *Puget Sound Business Journal.* Word is getting around about the Eastside's new industry. A journalist writing for Sweden's two largest computer magazines planned a quick stop on the Eastside as he toured U.S. software hot spots. Once he saw what was happening on the Eastside, however, he quickly changed his plans, cutting short some visits to other regions so he could stay longer. "He said he hadn't realized there were so many important companies in this area," said Fulton. "He was very excited. Some recent Japanese visitors said the same thing."

The Japanese visitors were familiar with at least one Eastside company—Nintendo of America Inc., which is a subsidiary of Nintendo Company Ltd. of

Japan. In 1987 its yearly sales exceeded $650 million, and by 1988 the Redmond company had become the world's leading manufacturer of video games, having captured 75 percent of the U.S. home video-game market.

Microsoft, meanwhile, has become the premier software company in the world and is setting the standards for the personal computer industry. Nestled in the woods of Redmond's Evergreen Place development, Microsoft has skyrocketed from a tiny operation in 1975 to a worldwide company whose sales could hit one billion dollars in 1990. The average age of the company's 3,000 employees is 31, illustrating why the Eastside has been referred to as a haven for the young and restless of the high-tech world.

Microsoft's stock more than quintupled in value within two years of the company going public in 1986. Its profits hit a robust $123.9 million in 1988, and in 1989 *Forbes* magazine listed it as the sixth most profitable company in the United States. The company's cofounder, Bill Gates, has found himself on the cover of such prestigious magazines as *Time* and *Business Week*. The dominant part of Micro-

soft's business has been "systems" software, which is software that tells the computer's hardware what to do. In 1988 systems software accounted for nearly half of the company's business. The same year, Microsoft opened the world's second largest software factory in Bothell.

Meanwhile, Boeing Computer Services (BCS), located in Bellevue's Cabot, Cabot & Forbes Business Park on I-90, has established itself as the Eastside's second largest private employer, providing jobs for some 2,500 people. It makes most of its money in support services for The Boeing Co., from whence it came. In

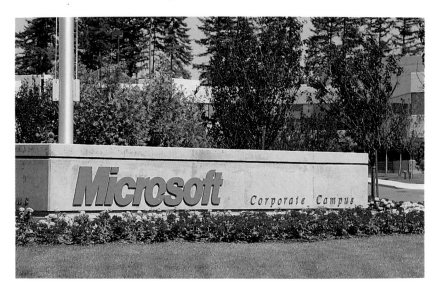

Microsoft's Corporate Campus is nestled in the woods of Redmond's Evergreen Place development. Photo by Gary Greene

total sales BCS became a billion-dollar-a-year company in 1987, although only roughly $250 million of that was from external business. Its biggest external customer is the federal government, and its single largest customer, NASA. Among other things, BCS runs the institutional computing in support of the Marshall Space Flight Center in Huntsville, Alabama, and is responsible for the communications system in support of the entire NASA operation. In the spring of 1988 it won a contract for the management information system that will link all the NASA sites involved with its planned space station, and all the contractors involved.

If such high-tech heavyweights dominate the business-page headlines, they're only the tip of the Eastside's iceberg. Microrim Inc. of Redmond, a spin-off from BCS in 1981, reported 1987 revenues of $20 million. At the time, it employed 160 people. The company provides data base management software and companion products for general business use. ESCA Corp. of Bellevue, which makes energy transfer regulation software for public utilities around the world, had revenues of $17.2 million and employed 239 people. Among the Eastside's other top software companies—all of Bellevue—were: Accountants Microsystems Inc. ($12 million in 1987 sales, 100 employees), Care Computer Systems Inc. ($6.4 million, 92 employees), Revelation Technologies ($5 million, 52 employees), and Custom Software Services ($2.9 million, 65 employees).

Such companies are causing some to predict even bigger things for the state's software industry in the future. In particular, the foreign market is expected to grow sharply; by 1991 U.S. software vendors are expected to reap $27 billion in overseas revenue, a 96 percent increase over 1988. And Washington State and the Eastside should get their share of that. The majority of Microsoft's sales eventually are expected to come from outside the U.S.

"In 2010 the software industry will be more important and bigger than Boeing," Bruce Milne, founder of the Washington Software Board, told *The Journal American*. That's a lofty statement. But Robert Fulton, now chairman of that board, believes it's possible.

"I see the day fast approaching when the national and international image of this state will be of a healthy, outdoorsy type of individual who's dressed in a Pacific Trail jacket and Reebok shoes. He'll be walking out of a Boeing 757 with a Douglas fir box under one armed filled with apples and a smoked salmon. Under the other arm will be a personal computer, and in the backpack—you guessed it— software from Washington State."

Beyond Software

If the software portion of the Eastside's high-tech industry involves an abundance of creativity, the rest of the area's high-tech industry is driven by the same kind of visionary thinking. A number of Eastside firms have earned national, and, in some cases, international, respect in the fields of communication, electronics, aerospace, biotechnology, medical equipment, and other areas.

Perhaps the fastest-growing segment of the non-software high-tech industry is biotechnology. The Puget Sound area has become one of the nation's leading areas for biotechnology research and development. The Eastside alone is home to more than 25 biotech companies. "The industry is booming beyond expectations," Robert Kupor, a nationally known biotech analyst, told *The Journal American*. The Puget Sound region is one of the dozen major centers for biotech in the U.S., according to *The Economist*, the prestigious London-based international news magazine.

One reason is the Health Sciences Center at the University of Washington, which is considered one of the leading research complexes in the nation for the study of human health, according to Alvin L. Kwiram, the university's senior vice provost. Among the Eastside's leaders in making medical devices is Advanced Technology Laboratories of Bothell, which makes medical diagnostic ultrasound and imaging equipment used in hospitals. In 1987 it had sales of $175 million and employed about 1,200 people.

Redmond-based Spacelabs ($117 million in 1987 sales, 400 Eastside employees) makes patient-monitoring systems that keep track of vital signs such as blood pressure, heartbeat, and breathing. Along with ATL, it is a subsidiary of Seattle-based Westmark International, the Puget Sound's fifth largest manufacturing employer. Physio-Control of Redmond ($100 million, 800 employees) makes acute cardiac care systems and monitoring systems for hospitals.

For perspective on the growth of the Eastside's biomedical field, one must look at the seemingly overnight high-tech development along I-405 near Bothell. In

1984 Snohomish County, in which most of The Technology Corridor is located, reported total employment in the biomed field as 200, excluding physicians and nurses. By the end of 1988 it was close to 2,000.

Washington's bid to strengthen its place in the world high-tech marketplace was buoyed in 1988 when ground was broken for a $15.9-million technology research and administrative facility for the Washington Technology Center on the UW campus. Much of private

Above: Patient-monitoring systems helped Spacelabs of Redmond achieve sales in 1987 alone in excess of $117 million. Photo by Jim Pickerell. Courtesy, TSW/ Click-Chicago, Ltd.

Left: The Koll North Creek business park development is located in Bothell on the I-405 high-tech corridor. Tech Center is a part of this development. Photo by Gary Greene

high-tech development comes as a spin-off from university research, and the center is expected to better focus UW's role in helping the industry. "With the University of Washington ranked [high] in the nation among public universities in receipt of federal research grants and one of the nation's most respected cancer research centers, the Fred Hutchinson, located here, Seattle has a little-known edge in biotechnology," said Roger Belanich, developer of Bothell's Canyon Park Business Center. "Japan's pharmaceutical firms are keenly interested in Seattle's burgeoning biotechnology industry."

While biotech companies flourish on I-90, other non-software high-tech companies continue to make their marks elsewhere on the Eastside. Among the giants is

Right: One reason for the success of biotechnology on the Eastside is the region's emphasis on research. A leading research institute for the area is the Health Sciences Center at the University of Washington. Photo by Jon Riley. Courtesy, TSW/Click-Chicago, Ltd.

Below: Cabot, Cabot and Forbes' I-90 Bellevue Business Park is home to Boeing Computer Services. BCS employs 2,500 Eastside residents. Photo by Gary Greene

Sundstrand, the Redmond company which was one of the first high-tech companies on the Eastside. Now employing some 1,500 people, Sundstrand makes circuit boards and avionics equipment, and is best known for producing the "black box" flight recorders for airplanes.

Another Redmond firm, Olin's Defense Systems Group, employs about 600 people and had 1987 sales of $50 million. The group consists of two local companies—Rocket Research and Pacific Electro Dynamics Inc. The latter makes, among other things, avionics and custom power supplies for aerospace, military, and commercial use. Rocket Research makes rocket engines for satellites and spacecraft, gas generators, munitions dispensing systems, and buoyancy and flotation devices.

Among the newer big-time high-tech firms on the Eastside is Esterline Corp., which had 1987 sales of $260 million. The company, a conglomerate that makes such products as printed circuit boards and specialty instruments, moved to Bellevue in 1987 from Darien, Connecticut, after a company shake-up.

Scores of smaller companies are making their presence known in the marketplace. They range from Kirkland-based Systi-Matic, which makes a state-of-the-art laser-cutting tool, to Bellevue-based Aiphone, which makes commercial intercom systems such as the ones found at the drive-through portions of fast-food restaurants. Together with the major companies on the Eastside, such firms are fortifying the Eastside's reputation as a national force on the high-tech frontier.

This attractive glass-and-steel office building is located in Bellevue on the I-90 business corridor. Bellevue is home to 154 high-tech firms. Photo by Gary Greene

5
AN ECONOMIC COLLAGE

P icture, if you will, a 35,000-pound Peterbilt truck next to a glass of Columbia Winery's chardonnay. A Boeing 747-400 next to a bottle of Coke. An industrial food-freezer system next to a Vernell's chocolate mint. Now you have an idea of the diverse products that help drive the Eastside economy, products as different in nature as they are in size. Some are large, some are small. Some are made on the Eastside, some are not. But all are part of an East-side economic collage that makes a collective statement of success.

The Eastside's economy is a collage whose most visible components may be high tech and high rises, but is composed of much, much more: regional distribution centers such as Safeway, telecommunications firms such as McCaw Cellular Communications, retail headquarters such as Costco Wholesale, financial institutions such as CityFed Mortgage, and manufacturing firms such as O'Brien Water Skis.

It is a collage filled with relatively small elements that often owe their existence to the larger elements. "Basically, the Eastside has two economic bases," said Bruce Baker, president of First Mutual Bank and chairman of the Bellevue Chamber of Commerce. "One is the corporations, top regional offices, and high-tech companies. The other is the service economy—the financial institutes, the law offices, consultants and CPAs who support those corporations, regional offices, and high-tech companies."

Beyond its heavy employment in high tech, the Eastside employs people in an array of other industries. *The Journal American*'s 1988 survey showed that 28,731 Eastsiders—one in five—work in retail trade; 12,714 in construction; 11,659 in wholesale trade; 10,597 in finance, insurance, and real estate; and 5,650 in manufacturing other than

With Boeing's arrival to the Eastside came a new vision of prosperity and growth which has since changed the face of Bellevue forever. Courtesy, TSW/Click-Chicago, Ltd

high tech. But interestingly, the company with the single largest influence on the Eastside's economy isn't even based here. It's the glue that holds the Eastside—and, for that matter, the entire Puget Sound region—together. It's The Boeing Co.

The Boeing Influence

In the 1950s and 1960s The Boeing Co. was the catalyst that turned Bellevue from a stump farm into suburbia. New neighborhoods such as Lake Hills and Newport Hills were so thick with Boeing engineers that Bellevue had the air of a company town; so what if the company's plants were in Seattle, Renton, Kent, and Everett. Now, even though the area has diversified with an array of new businesses, Boeing remains the economic backbone of Bellevue and the Eastside. Some 12,000 Eastsiders—one of every 12 employed adults—work for The Boeing Co. Of those, roughly 2,500 work at Boeing Computer Services in Bellevue.

Each year the Seattle company's payroll alone pumps hundreds of millions of dollars into the Eastside economy, most of which will be spent at Eastside businesses. Anyone skeptical of Boeing's influence on the Eastside economy need only try finding a parking space at Bellevue Square the day after Boeing has issued a holiday bonus; their 1988 gift averaged $1,327 per employee. "Boeing is the leading reason for our economic vitality," said Kemper Freeman, Jr., the Bellevue native who redeveloped Bellevue Square and built Bellevue Place. "How many restaurants, supermarkets, banks, attorneys, and accountant firms wouldn't exist if it wasn't for Boeing? A lot."

In addition to employment, Boeing influences the Eastside through spin-off business. As the saying goes, "When Boeing sneezes, everyone else catches cold." Beyond Boeing Computer Services, where 80 percent of sales go to support The Boeing Co., a substantial number of Eastside companies supply products and services to Boeing, companies such as Sundstrand Data and Pacific Electro Dynamics of Redmond and Criton Technologies of Bellevue. "If Boeing does well, suppliers to Boeing do well," Randy C. James, Seafirst vice chairman and manager of the commercial markets group, told *The Journal American*. "If suppliers to Boeing do well, then all the service industries do well—the grocery stores do well, clothing stores do well."

And Boeing is doing very well indeed. Riding the biggest boom in aviation history, the world's leader in the aerospace industry was the nation's second largest exporter in 1987, trailing only General Motors. Roughly one-quarter of its business is in the military and space fields, up from about 15 percent in 1980. Boeing, which employs 153,000 people worldwide, broke records each year from 1985 through 1988 for total commercial jet orders. By late 1988 it was selling them at the rate of $85 million worth a day.

Manufacturing

Eddie Bauer Inc. of Redmond sold $150 million worth of outdoor wear and sporting goods in 1987. Vernell's Fine Candies of Bellevue satisfied candy lovers to the tune of $30 million the same year.

But when it comes to non-high-tech manufacturing on the Eastside, the grand-daddy of them all is Bellevue-based PAC-CAR, whose top products are Peterbilt and Kenworth trucks. With 1988 revenues of $3.1 billion, PACCAR—the Eastside's lone *Fortune* 500 company (143rd on the list)—had more than three times the sales of software giant Microsoft. The truck manufacturing itself is done in Seattle, Renton, and around the country, but the company's corporate offices are in the Bellevue Business Center building, where 350 of its 14,000 employees work.

Beyond PACCAR, other top Eastside manufacturing firms include Bellevue-based Pacific Coca-Cola; Redmond-based Genie Industries, which makes portable lifting equipment; Redmond-based Frigoscandia, which produces industrial food-freezing systems and water-jet cutting

Like its sister truck, PACCAR's Peterbilt, the Kenworth truck has been crucial to the success of American trucking for generations. Photo by Mark E. Gibson

tools; and Bellevue-based Olympic Stain, which sells more oil-based stain than any company in the world.

A Potpourri of Products and Services

About every 10 minutes, day and night, a semi-truck rolls out of the Safeway Distribution Center in Bellevue's Bel-Red industrial district, en route to deliver products to one of the 181 Safeway stores in the Northwest. The significance to the Eastside? Safeway's Bellevue-based Seattle Division employs more people—1,500—than any other private Eastside company except for Microsoft, Boeing Computer Services, and Sundstrand Data.

As Safeway's trucks rumble in and out of their Bellevue base, other Eastside companies are rolling along, too. From engineering to electricity, financial services to fireworks, the area's varied businesses add a dimension of diversity to the Eastside's economy.

Among the leaders is CH2M HILL, the Northwest's largest general-engineering firm. The Bellevue operation is the regional headquarters and largest office of the Corvallis, Oregon-based CH2M HILL, the nation's fifth largest architecture-engineering firm. Among companies that do engineering only, the privately held company is the largest. Some 400 people work in its regional headquarters in Bellevue's Security Pacific Plaza, where projects have ranged from Bellevue's N.E. 4th Street-Interstate 405 interchange to a commercial rocket launch facility in Hawaii.

Among the Eastside's oldest firms is Puget Sound Power & Light Company, an electric utility that began business back in 1912. In 1956 the company erected a four-story, $2-million structure in downtown Bellevue that some still consider the city's first "high rise." The company had 1987 revenues of $729 million, making it the eighth largest publicly owned company in the state, according to the *Puget Sound Business Journal*. It employs 2,414 people, 873 in Bellevue.

Two telecommunications companies, McCaw Cellular Communications and U S West/New Vector, have added greatly to the Eastside's business mix. McCaw, which is located in the new Carillon Point development in Kirkland, had a market value of $2.4 billion in April 1988, making *Business Week*'s Top 1,000 list (235th). Meanwhile, U S West/New Vector, a downtown Bellevue company that went public in April 1988, had a market value of about one billion dollars at that time.

In 1987 United Parcel Service opened its largest shipping station in the Northwest in Redmond. When running at maximum capacity, the $21-million facility can operate 300 trucks and move 20,000 packages a day. UPS employs 325 people at its Redmond facility.

Washington's wine industry has risen to national prominence in the last decade—only California and New York produce more wine than the Evergreen State—and the Eastside has played an integral part in that climb. Three of the state's top 10 wine producers are located on the Eastside. Chateau Ste. Michelle, based in Woodinville, is by far the state's largest producer, shipping 570,000 cases in 1987. In 1988 it became the first non-California winery to be named "Best of the Best American Wineries" by *Wine and Country* magazine and later was chosen "Winery of the Year" by the national Tasters Guild. Columbia Winery, which became a next-door neighbor of Ste. Michelle's in the Sammamish Valley in 1988 after years in Bellevue, is the state's sixth largest. Snoqualmie Winery, based in Snoqualmie, is ranked ninth.

Meanwhile, scores of other companies add to the variety of non-manufacturing business on the Eastside. Among them: VWR, a Bellevue-based distributor of printing and laboratory supplies; Penwest, a national grain-processing firm whose corporate headquarters are in Bellevue; Ace Novelty, a Bellevue distributor of fireworks; and Sporting Edge, a Bothell-based catalog company that offers high-tech home accessories ranging from talking scales to cedar-filled dog hammocks.

Foreign Investment, Foreign Trade

As the Eastside's prominence has grown, so too has the offshore interest in the area. In 1988 more than 60 Eastside companies were wholly or partly owned by foreign investors, according to Washington's Trade and Economic Development Division. The statistics reflect a surge in foreign investment being enjoyed by the state as a whole. More than 300 foreign-owned establishments were located in Washington in 1988, an investment that exceeded one billion dollars. The foreign companies employed more than 23,000 state residents.

On the Eastside the growth in foreign investment has been dramatic. Before 1970 only about 10 foreign-owned companies existed in the area. That number tripled in the next decade, and has doubled since then. The largest companies on the Eastside that are wholly owned by foreign corporations are Redmond-based Nintendo (Japan), which makes video games and employs some 225 people; Unisea (Japan), a Redmond seafood processing company that employs 200; Almac Electronics (United Kingdom), a Bellevue electronics firm that employs 120; and Helly-Hansen (Norway), a Redmond outdoor-wear company that employs 120.

Foreign investment in the Eastside has culminated in, among other things, the development of Bellevue Place. Photo by Gary Greene

In terms of development, at least two major Eastside projects have received foreign backing. Three Japanese companies were major investors in the $150-million first phase of Bellevue Place in downtown Bellevue, and a Korean conglomerate joined Swanson-Dean Corp. as a partner in the completion of Providence Point, an upscale retirement community near Issaquah.

Meanwhile, foreign trade has become one of the fastest-growing areas of the Pacific Northwest economy. In the past decade foreign commerce passing through the Northwest more than tripled, rising to a record $43 billion. No other state, for instance, does more trade with China than Washington. As world trade continues to expand, and Asian nations capture an increasing portion of that trade, Pacific Northwest ports will benefit. And the Eastside stands to benefit because of its proximity to Seattle's port, which handles 30 percent of West Coast cargo. Realizing as much, the Greater Redmond Chamber of Commerce sent a contingent, including U.S. Senator Rod Chandler, to Japan in 1987 to make business contacts.

In late 1988 Rupert Pennant-Rea, the editor-in-chief of *The Economist* magazine, told a Seattle audience that the Pacific Northwest was in an ideal position to become a strong force in the world economy. Pennant-Rea's reasoning was based on everything from the region's relatively even mix of economic activity to its ability to bounce back from economic adversity, as it did after the Boeing bust of the late 1960s and early 1970s. "Finally, I would look for a place that was attractive to live in," rich with mountains, clean water, and clean air. "And I would say, lucky Pacific Northwest," for having such things, added Pennant-Rea.

Retail

Mention retail sales on the Eastside and thoughts rivet to Bellevue Square. With 1987 revenues of $957 million, some one-third of Bellevue's retail sales, such attention is justified. But Bellevue Square isn't the only game in town—or across the Eastside.

A number of retail companies base their operations on the Eastside. Among them are Bellevue-based Quality Food Centers (1,500 employees), Kirkland-based Costco Wholesale (1,400), Bellevue-based Mervyn's (1,125), Bellevue-based Lamonts Apparel Inc. (1,000), Bellevue-based Schuck's Auto Supply (700), and Redmond-based Pay Less Drug Stores (614).

Four major malls anchor the Eastside. Beyond Bellevue Square, others are Factoria Square, Crossroads Mall, and Totem Lake Shopping Center. The Bellevue Overlake area has blossomed into a major attraction, with Sears as its anchor. Kirkland boasts five-year-old Kirkland Park Place. And in Issaquah, Gilman Village, a cluster of historic homes that have been refurbished as shops, gives the city a shopping

In addition to Bellevue Square, Factoria Square, the Crossroads, and the Totem Lake shopping centers are the major malls in the Eastside area. Photo by Gary Greene

appeal unique to the Eastside. The village, which exudes a country feel, is the city's top source of sales-tax revenue.

If the Eastside's existing retail outlets exude a certain vibrancy, the blueprints suggest more is on the way. In March 1988 Redmond approved the Town Center shopping complex which backers see as a focal point for downtown Redmond. The complex, to be developed by the Winmar Co., is expected to include an eight-story hotel, an eight-screen movie complex, four department stores, office buildings, and 120 to 150 specialty shops.

Meanwhile, Bothell is forging ahead with plans to revitalize its downtown with hopes of attracting more shoppers. It isn't alone. Not satisfied with its retail draw, Kirkland in October 1988 unanimously approved a new business improvement district for the downtown area. Studies had shown that 80 percent of all Kirkland residents do most of their shopping outside the city. An upgraded downtown, business leaders are hoping, will change those statistics. So should the addition of Carillon Point, a plush, new, mixed-used development on Lake Washington. The Skinner Development Company project includes a hotel, restaurant, marina, shops, parks, and condominiums.

Commercial Real Estate

An aerial map of an Eastside business park hangs from the wall in Tom Bernard's downtown Bellevue office. The Eastside land developer and former chairman of the Bellevue Chamber of Commerce has to have the photo reshot every year because of the dramatic changes in the park. Eastside commercial real estate has boomed in the 1980s. Part of that boom, of course, has occurred in downtown Bellevue, which has emerged as a major-league urban center. But a good portion has occurred along freeways and nestled in forested office parks, fueled by the rise of the high-tech industry.

"Downtown is visible and everybody oohs and ahs, but it's certainly not the whole enchilada," said Robert C. Wallace, founder and managing partner of Wallace Properties Group in Bellevue, and, like Bernard, a former Bellevue Chamber of Commerce chairman.

Statistically, the increases are mind-boggling. In 1975 the Eastside had 500,000 square feet of office space. By 1987 it had 13 million square feet, 26 times as much. This growth is reflected in the soaring membership of the Puget Sound chapter of the National Association of Office and Industrial Parks. In the mid-1970s, said Bernard, it had eight members. It now has over 250. It is significant, Kemper Freeman, Jr., points out, that the Eastside kept pace with Seattle during the 1980s in terms of office-space absorption. "But what's even more significant is that those were the best eight years in Seattle's history," he said.

Why the explosion of commercial real estate on the Eastside? The reasons are many. In the late 1970s, the growth resulted partly from downtown Seattle business owners and managers deciding they no longer wanted to fight the commuter traffic to Seattle, according to Ronald Leibsohn, president of Leibsohn & Co., a Bellevue-based commercial real estate brokerage firm. Meanwhile, the Eastside was realizing the benefits of growth. "People were realizing that if the economic pie is bigger, everyone gets a bigger piece," said Bernard.

In the 1960s Bert McNae began developing the Overlake area of what is now northeast Bellevue and south Redmond. In the early 1970s The Koll Company began development of the Eastside's first "incubator" business park near and along 148th Avenue N.E., near State Route 520. The Koll Overlake project evolved as the largest on the Eastside. Soon, traditional "woody walkup" business centers gave way to larger, more sophisticated business parks. Cabot, Cabot & Forbes established its I-90/Bellevue Business Park in 1978. Boeing Computer Service anchored the park in 1980.

In the early 1980s several major corporations in Seattle decided to open branch offices or expand satellite offices in the area. They chose the Eastside. Since 1983 the driving force has been high tech—and the companies that arrived to service the high-tech companies. In the 1980s many of Seattle's major law firms, accounting firms, and financial service companies established themselves on the Eastside.

Meanwhile, many of the high-tech companies outgrew their first Eastside homes. "No sooner had companies entered into a five-year lease than they found their needs outgrowing their space," wrote Leibsohn in the *Puget Sound Business Journal.* "This resulted in moves every two or three years, accompanied by further growth."

In 1986, for example, Microsoft moved from a Bellevue location along State Route 520 to a six-building headquarters in Redmond's forested Evergreen Place development. Only two years later it added two more buildings on its 30-acre site, moved its support center to Bellevue's Lincoln Plaza, and opened a 265,000-square-foot manufacturing assembly and distribution facility in Bothell. In 1988 Generic Software Inc. left a 14,000-square-foot building in Redmond's Willows Road area to lease an entire 41,000-square-foot building in the Quadrant Business Park in Bothell.

During the 1980s, two-thirds of the Eastside's office-space growth was due to self-incubation—start-up businesses, expanding businesses, or spin-off businesses. The rest were businesses that moved to the Eastside from outside the area. The developers who built most of that office space were Kemper Development Co., The Vyzis Co., Cabot, Cabot & Forbes, The Koll Company, and Wright Runstad & Co.

Beyond downtown Bellevue, which represents roughly one-fourth of Eastside office space, the region has a number of hot spots. The Interstate 90 Corridor, for example, has enough buildings on the blueprints to add 5 million square feet of office and other space by 1995—the equivalent of four 76-story Columbia Center buildings. The I-90 Corridor, which now stretches from Factoria to Issaquah, is already home to such companies as Boeing Computer Services. The Newport Corporate Center is the latest major addition on I-90. The center, which opened in 1988, includes the seven-story, pink-glassed Newport Tower, described by its developer, Basil Vyzis, as an urban building in suburbia.

If I-90 is hot, however, the I-405 Technology Corridor may be even hotter. The 10-mile corridor, a swath stretching from Mukilteo south to Bothell, includes three major Eastside business centers: Canyon Park, Koll North Creek, and Quadrant Business Park. Roughly 83 percent of the companies are high tech in nature. In an uncommon approach, five development businesses joined forces to undertake a national and international marketing effort to attract new industry. Traditionally, this type of economic development has been left to local, state, or federal governments.

Begun in 1985, by mid-1988 The Corridor boasted 50 high-tech firms, many involved in biomedical technology and computer products and services. When built to full capacity, The Corridor is expected to boast 19 million square feet, 34,000 new

jobs, and a capital investment of $2.9 million.

Among the swankier sites for non-downtown office space is Carillon Point, a mixed-used development on Kirkland's Lake Washington waterfront that opened in August 1989. Besides 467,000 square feet of office space, the development includes a hotel, marina, restaurant, retail shops, and condominiums—all sharing a spectacular waterfront site.

Beyond major companies, the Eastside is attracting scores of smaller companies, many of whom are moving into full-service small-business centers. Eight such centers opened in Bellevue in a 12-month period between 1987 and 1988, a 47 percent annual increase, according to the *Puget Sound Business Journal.* By June 1988 Bellevue had 25 centers compared to Seattle's 11. "Seattle has the national name recognition but Bellevue offers greater mobility, is less confusing to get around in, better planned, and closer to housing," said Sherry Wilson, who owns three Eastside business centers and expects more to form in Issaquah, Kirkland, Redmond, and Bothell.

About half her tenants are local professionals, such as attorneys, consultants, and advertising executives. The other half are high-tech marketing reps from California computer firms, yet another reminder of how the Eastside's high-tech business has become a magnet for growth in the 1980s.

Residential Real Estate

Back in the 1870s, Bellevue's first land buyer, William Meydenbauer, sold his Meydenbauer Bay property to a gentleman named Charles Kittenger for the hefty sum of $50 an acre. Ten years later Meydenbauer tried to buy it back but balked when Kittenger wanted $75. Times have changed. Now some Eastside properties in that area are deemed so valuable that developers will pay up to $500,000—then have the house bulldozed to make room for a new house that might range from $500,000 to well over one million dollars.

Such cases aren't widespread, but they do reflect the value of Eastside property—and the demand for that property. In this case the attraction was Lake Washington waterfront property with a view. But that's just one type of property that has helped make the Eastside residential real estate market one of the strongest in the Northwest.

Eighty-five percent of new construction in King County in the 1980s has occurred on the Eastside, according to Hebert Research Inc. On the Eastside's "east side"—the Sammamish Plateau area—new home developments have sprouted like spring flowers. The entire Eastside grew 18.1 percent in 1980—amazing in itself—but King County's East Sammamish area (east of Lake Sammamish) grew 58 percent and Bear Creek (east of Redmond) grew 39 percent. Naturally, such growth has meant big business for the construction and real estate industries.

Klahanie, a planned community on the plateau developed by Lowe Enterprises Northwest of Bellevue, averaged a phenomenal five sales per week—about 1,000 total—from the time it opened in May 1985 through May 1989. In 1988, 19 of the top 25 single-family home builders in Puget Sound were based on the Eastside, according to a *Puget Sound Business Journal* survey. The leader, Conner Development Company of Bellevue, built 187 houses—$28 million worth—in 1987 alone. Meanwhile, four of Puget Sound's top seven residential real estate firms were based on the East-

Facing page: The Newport Corporate Center, developed by Basil Vyzis, opened in 1988. It is the latest major addition on I-90. Photo by Gary Greene

side: John L. Scott Inc., Coldwell Banker Residential Real Estate, Richard James Realtors, and Wallace and Wheeler Inc. Those four alone employed more than 1,500 licensed agents.

By 1988 King County's growth became so focused on the Eastside that the county's Building and Land Division moved its headquarters and 240 employees to a complex between Factoria and Eastgate.

Financial Institutes

By 1987 Bellevue was second only to Seattle as a regional center for financial, insurance, and service companies, according to John Valaas, senior vice president at Seafirst's corporate banking division. "The economy in the Puget Sound area, as a
whole, has grown," Valaas told the *Daily Journal of Commerce.* "This has led various elements of the service center, such as law offices, banks and accounting firms, to
open major offices in Bellevue as well [as Seattle.]"

The anchor positions in downtown high rises held by CityFed Mortgage, Security Pacific Bank, and Seafirst Bank suggest the importance financial institutes place
on the Eastside. "The Eastside is a critical market for us," said Valaas. "That is

where the battles of the future will be waged."

Signs that others agree are everywhere. SAFECO Life Insurance Company, which already has a regional office in Redmond, is planning to move its corporate offices—and some 625 employees—from Seattle to Redmond in 1990. Allstate Insurance, meanwhile, plans to move its regional center and some 550 to 600 employees from Seattle to Bothell's North Creek Valley the same year. In addition, the Northwest's largest venture capital firm, Cable & Howse Ventures, is based in Bellevue. By mid-1988 Cable & Howse had more than $160 million under management in 98 companies.

Tourism and Convention Business

From Kirkland's new tour-boat business to the showery spray of Snoqualmie Falls, the Eastside attracts thousands of tourists each year. Thousands more come to the Eastside on business. In Bellevue alone, conventions create more than $40 million

Cyclists test their skill in Redmond's velodrome. Photo by Gary Greene

worth of business per year, according to the King County Convention and Visitors Bureau. The average convention draws 150 delegates, who spend an average of $100 per day. With the addition of Bellevue Place's Hyatt Regency, Bellevue now has six hotels and 1,117 rooms. Including tourists, visitors in Bellevue spent $135 million in 1986 alone.

Among the drawing cards are Bellevue Square, wineries, Kirkland's waterfront, Redmond's velodrome, Issaquah's Gilman Village, nearby ski resorts, and the area's parks and lakes. Lake Sammamish State Park, with 1.6 million visitors in 1986, was second only to the Kingdome as the leading attraction in the county. Kirkland's new tour-boat business, christened in 1988, could eventually bring $2 million a year in tourist dollars to the Eastside, according to the state Department of Commerce and Economic Development.

Although the Eastside isn't a major tourist destination like Seattle or Victoria, British Columbia, the region still benefits significantly from the many first-rate Pacific Northwest attractions, be they in the area of sports, culture, or outdoors. Among the event drawing cards in recent years: the Final Four NCAA basketball championships in Seattle in 1984 and 1989, the "Son of Heaven: Imperial

Arts of China" exhibit in Seattle in 1988, and the World's Fair in Vancouver, British Columbia, in 1986. The 1990 Goodwill Games, to be held in Seattle (with bicycle racing in Redmond), provide yet another potentially big draw for the Eastside.

The Eastside's variety of attractions continues to expand. By late 1988 Snoqualmie Winery was planning extensive expansion of resort and recreation facilities that included a 15,000-seat open-air amphitheater and a 250-seat restaurant. Ste. Michelle, meanwhile, has already established a tradition of blending fine wine and fine music. On warm summer afternoons, when the sound of bluegrass music drifts across the grounds, the scene symbolizes the alluring mixture of business and pleasure that has come to distinguish the Eastside.

An important part of the Bellevue plan has been the establishment and maintenance of some of the county's finest parks, including Kelsey Creek Park. Photo by Gary Greene

Above: A rainbow-colored parachute is the hit of the party at this gathering in Lake Sammamish State Park in Issaquah. Photo by Gary Greene

Left: Residents today, like never before, are in a position to enjoy what the Eastside has to offer both in terms of business and pleasure. Photo by Eric Draper

6
SERVING THE EASTSIDE

E ach month nearly 1,000 people drive into an Eastside neighborhood, unload their life's possessions, and call this place
home. Why here? Jobs, of course, are a major reason; as
the last three chapters pointed out, a strong economy
draws newcomers like a magnet. But there's more—much
more—to the Eastside's appeal than simply attractive employment and business opportunities. There are such factors as
school systems that annually rank among the state's best, first-
class health-care facilities, and low crime rates. Here's a look at
some of the services provided by the Eastside—and how those
services contribute to the high quality of life found throughout
the region.

Schools

When it comes to public schools, the Eastside and Seattle have
gradually undergone a role reversal in recent decades. At one
time, one of the things that kept some Seattleites from moving
to the Eastside was the latter's weak school systems. Now, the
reason many Seattleites are moving to the Eastside is, in part, because of those same school systems—now that Eastside
schools have been become among the best in the state.

"In many respects, Seattle's loss has been to the Eastside's benefit," said James Hebert of Hebert Research Inc.
"Seattle's schools have deteriorated significantly. What that's
done is prompt a lot of families to relocate to the Eastside, particularly many of those in the young professional group."

The numbers help tell the story: In 1989 a report released
by the governor's task force showed high dropout rates for Seattle's 10 high schools, ranging from 23 to 48 percent. Meanwhile, all but one of the 14 Eastside high schools had rates of
less than 15 percent. And of the state's schools with the

Serving the Presbyterian community of the Eastside, the warm and elegant architecture of the First Presbyterian Church creates an inspiring setting for worship. Photo by Gary Greene

Newport High School was among the 10 Washington State schools with the lowest dropout rates. Photo by Gary Greene

lowest dropout rates, four of the top 10 belonged to Eastside high schools—Liberty High and Issaquah High in Issaquah, and Newport High and Interlake High in Bellevue.

In addition, state test scores clearly point to the Eastside's quality public educational system. The four big Eastside school districts ranked 10 to 30 percentile points above statewide Metropolitan Achievement Test scores, according to a 1987 report. The national average, based on standardized tests given at three grade levels, was 50. Washington State's was 56. But Bellevue, Issaquah, Lake Washington, and Northshore school districts combined for a 68 average. Beyond that, the districts offer a host of special programs for the gifted and those with special learning needs.

Administrators say the higher socioeconomic and professional status of Eastside families, coupled with a strong family emphasis on education, give Eastside students more motivation to succeed. Eastside adults tend to be well educated. For example, nationally, 17 percent of adults have at least 16 years of education; in Bellevue, 41 percent do.

An experienced staff also plays a big role in Bellevue's success. The average Bellevue teacher has 20 years experience. Almost 50 percent hold advanced degrees. And yet, the district maintains a forward-thinking spirit more often associated with a younger staff. Among Bellevue's most recent innovative moves has been "school-centered decision making," a decentralized system of management. Started in 1988, the program—believed to be a first of its kind in the U.S.—creates partnerships among staff, parents, and students to reach consensus on decisions that effect the quality of the educational programs.

There is much quality on which to build. In 1987-1988, test scores in the Bellevue School District were the highest in the state for school districts with enrollments of greater than 7,000. Some 428 graduating seniors won scholarships and awards, 35 were National Merit-commended students, and 13 were National Merit semifinalists. On the elementary level the district's Phantom Lake school was among only 10 schools nationwide to receive the President's Environmental Youth Award for its salmon-stocking project. And Cherry Crest Elementary was chosen as one of two outstanding public schools in Washington.

Similar awards have been bestowed upon schools in other Eastside districts over the last few years. For example, in 1984 the Lake Washington School District's Redmond High was selected by the U.S. Department of Education as among the nation's best high schools. Rose Hill Junior High, meanwhile, has produced the nation's best junior high school jazz band four of the five years from 1983 to 1988, according to *down beat* magazine, which annually judges taped performances.

Lake Washington, a fractured district in the early 1970s with little public support, has developed into a district so highly respected that in a survey of 100 state school superintendents, 62 ranked it tops. Reflecting its forward-looking approach to education, Lake Washington's 2001 Program has already resulted in over 1,500 computers being made available to students. More than 1,000 district employees have earned computers for their personal use by enrolling in an innovative district computer program. Given such progressive programs, it's not surprising that more than three-quarters of the district's high school graduates continue on to attend two- or four-year colleges.

Next door, the Northshore School District has earned accolades of its own. In the 1986-1987 and 1987-1988 school years, a district principal and teacher each won state "Awards for Excellence." In 1987 the district's school board was named the outstanding school board in the state. In addition, the district's 2.17 percent high school dropout rate ranks among the state's lowest.

Eastside children can be proud of the fact that theirs are some of the finest schools in the nation. Photo by Eric Draper

Such honors and statistics help explain why the district got such a favorable response in a survey of the community. Of those asked, 86 percent said they considered Northshore education "well above average" and 35 percent regarded it as "excellent." So coveted are Northshore teaching jobs that an average of 100 applications are received for each opening.

Among the feathers in the cap of the 7,400-student Issaquah School District was the 1988 honoring of Clark Elementary as one of Washington's "Schools for the 21st Century." The Learning Community, a program that brings moms and dads into the classroom, has transformed Issaquah's oldest elementary school into a model for the future.

In terms of athletics, Eastside public

high schools have won more than a dozen state championships during the 1980s and consistently have students placing high in national debate, math, and science contests.

Beyond public schools, the Eastside offers an array of private institutes catering to different needs and tastes. Among them are Bellevue Christian School, founded in 1950 and among the region's older private schools; Eastside Catholic, a coed high school; Forest Ridge, an all-girls Catholic school whose campus sits on Somerset Hill; and Overlake School, a prep school where 98 percent of the school's students have gone on to college.

Higher Education

Bellevue Community College (BCC), which celebrates its 25th year on the Eastside in 1991, serves more students—12,530—than any other higher-education institute in western Washington except for the University of Washington. Loosely known as "the Harvard of two-year colleges," BCC's thrust is academic education. Nearly half of all its students (49 percent) take academic transfer classes with the intention of finishing their degrees at four-year schools. That's a higher percentage than any other community college in western Washington.

"I'm overwhelmed by what BCC means to the Eastside," said Laurie Full-Ray, who serves on the college's Foundation board of directors. "The caliber of the people there is great. People don't realize the impact of the college."

Among its drawing cards is a "contracting" system—offering classes totally financed by students. This gives the college the opportunity to offer more sections of heavily demanded classes than the state-allocated funds generally allow. In addition, BCC offers "Second Chance Scholarships" to students with high potential but mediocre high school grades.

In June 1987, 215 of 266 recent graduates were employed in jobs related to their education. BCC works closely with Eastside businesses in setting up continuing education programs. In addition, in 1988 it began offering its first off-campus classes, at Redmond High.

Three other institutes, each with a different focus, contribute to the Eastside's upper-level education:

—Lake Washington Vocational Technical Institute, located in Kirkland, trains technicians and skilled workers for business, health, service, and industrial occupations in the Greater Seattle area. The state-supported school is a natural link between employers who need skilled workers and people who need good jobs. Because the school is tax-supported, the cost of training is surprisingly low.

The bottom line at the school isn't credits, but graduates who get jobs. More than 96 percent of recent graduates found jobs in their new career fields within 90 days of graduation, according to the most recent State of Washington follow-up report. The school enrolls more than 28,000 people each year in areas ranging from culinary arts to computer drafting. The VocTech also provides customized training programs for business and industry.

—City University, an independent institute, aims to provide educational opportunities to segments of the population not reached by traditional means. Founded in 1973, it is geared toward working adults, with classes offered during the daytime, evenings, and weekends. In addition, it offers the Distance Learning Program, an indepen-

Lake Washington Vocational Technical Institute in Kirkland trains students to be technicians and skilled workers for business, health, service, and industrial occupations in the Greater Seattle area. Photo by Gary Greene

dent study project designed to allow students to work at home, on the job, or on the road. The undergraduate and graduate programs focus on business administration and management. While based in Bellevue, City University has expanded to provide instruction throughout the state, as well as in Oregon, California, British Columbia, and Zurich, Switzerland.

—Northwest College, located in Kirkland, is a four-year Assemblies of God school which dates from 1934. It offers a Bible-based education with a strong emphasis on mission work. The college has sent more than 350 missionaries to every continent and countless pastors to churches throughout the U.S. The school's 55-acre campus is also home to the Seattle Seahawks football team, which leased land from the school in 1986 to construct its plush training and meeting facility.

—Griffin College, located in downtown Bellevue, offers classes in an array of business-related fields, from office administration to computer programming, from electronics technology to travel and airlines.

The future promises more improvements in higher education on the Eastside. In May 1989 the Washington State legislature approved funding for a degree-granting branch of the University of Washington in the Bothell-Woodinville area. The campus will serve upper division and graduate students. The Bellevue Chamber of Commerce provided staff support and volunteer leadership to the Eastside Higher Education Coalition, the organization that lobbied for the branch campus. The coalition is made up of concerned businesses, organizations, and individuals.

Health Care

The growth of health-care facilities on the Eastside aptly reflects the rags-to-riches development of the region. It took more than seven years to raise the money for Overlake Hospital in Bellevue, now known as Overlake Hospital Medical Center. The fund-raising campaign included everything from bake sales to a grudge golf match between Kemper Freeman, Sr., and his rival, James Ditty (Ditty won). But in October 1960 the 52-bed hospital opened its doors and, in a sense, opened the doors to an array of new, quality health care on the Eastside.

Today the not-for-profit hospital has four times as many beds as it originally did, a Level II trauma center, an $11-million surgical pavilion, and an outpatient surgery facility that is one of the largest on the West Coast. In 1988 Overlake successfully performed more than 200 open-heart surgeries, the type of operation performed only at downtown Seattle hospitals until July 1987.

A national demonstration project was done at Overlake that same year by the American Association of Critical-Care Nurses. The findings? The average patient mortality rate in Overlake's intensive care and critical care units was nearly 50 percent below predicted rates, based on nationally recognized formulas. In addition, the overall cost of care was significantly lower than figures for hospitals of similar scope.

If Overlake was the first major health-care facility on the Eastside, it wasn't the last. Evergreen Hospital Medical Center opened in Kirkland in 1972 after residents of Kirkland, Juanita, Bothell, Woodinville, and Kenmore banded together to provide health-care services for northeast King County. The 134-bed hospital specializes in obstetrics and maternity care, cancer care, cardiac care, emergency care, orthopedics, and surgery. In 1988 Evergreen became the first hospital in the state to use a laser-surgery technique for vascular surgery. In 1991 the hospital plans to open the Evergreen Hospice Center, which will provide compassionate

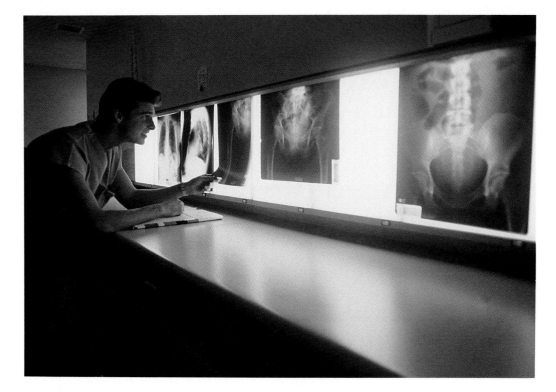

An intern reviews X-rays at the Overlake Hospital Medical Center. Photo by Eric Draper

care to the dying and their families. The hospice was given overwhelming support in 1988 when a $4.4-million bond issue was passed.

Group Health, the Northwest's largest health maintenance organization, opened a 167-bed hospital in Redmond in 1977. The average stay at the hospital is 3.9 days, lowest of all Group Health facilities and lower than all hospitals statewide, which average 5.2 days. Group Health will coordinate medical needs for the athletes at the 1990 Goodwill Games in Seattle.

The Eastside's newest hospital, Snoqualmie Valley, opened in 1983. The hospital's relatively small size—28 beds—promotes more personalized care and its location affords a sweeping view of the Cascades. Some 125 physicians and 30 registered nurses serve the hospital.

Beyond hospitals, the Eastside is blessed with a number of medical clinics, many of them spin-offs from Seattle hospitals. The Eastside's medic teams have proven to be first-class. In Bellevue, for example, the chance of surviving a heart attack is more than twice the national rate. Dr. Jack Ciliberti, medical director of Bellevue's paramedic program and director of Overlake's emergency department, attributes this success to Bellevue paramedics' low turnover rate and the pool of experienced emergency medical technicians. "We think we have the best resuscitation rate in the world," Ciliberti said.

A Safe Place

When the latest edition of *Safe Places for the '80s* was published in 1984, only one community in the state of Washington made David and Holly Franke's list: Clyde Hill, a community of 3,000 people that abuts Bellevue's northwestern boundary. While the rest of the Eastside is more susceptible to crime, it still has a relatively low rate. Back when Bellevue was a smaller community, it, too, was listed among the 46 safest places to live in the U.S. in an earlier edition of the book. Although crime has naturally risen with the increase in population, the city—and the Eastside as a whole—has avoided the "big-time crime" that has plagued so many areas of America.

"People who move in here from out of state—back East or the L.A./San Francisco area, for example—think this is paradise," said Lieutenant Bob Wuorenma of Bellevue's crime prevention unit. "This is nothing compared to what they're used to."

In 1987, for example, Bellevue, Redmond, and Kirkland combined had only one murder. In fact, the total number of major crimes was down in all three Eastside cities. Bellevue police said one big reason was attentive residents. "We've worked a lot of years to get the community and the police working together," Major Paul Olsen of the Bellevue Police told *The Journal American*. "People are educating themselves."

In 1988 crime levels across the Eastside were generally down from the previous year and well below the area's peak years of 1981 and 1982.

Communications

The media has begun to recognize the growing importance of the Eastside. In 1975 Seattle television stations rarely paid much attention to life on the eastern side of Lake Washington. Nor did Seattle's two major dailies, the *Times* and *P-I*. At the time, two weekly newspapers, Kirkland's *Eastside Journal* and *The Bellevue American*, were the main sources of local news for Eastside residents.

Fifteen years has changed everything. For starters, the two weeklies were acquired by Longview Publishing Company and merged into a single newspaper in 1976—*The Journal American*. It was the first new daily paper in Washington since 1947. "I don't think most people figured it would last a year," Bill Lagen, a former Bellevue city councilman, told *The Journal American* in 1986 when the paper celebrated its 10-year anniversary. As it has matured, *The J-A* has helped the Eastside develop an identity all its own. "There wouldn't be an Eastside without *The J-A*," said Lagen.

In 1986 Longview Publishing president John McClelland, Jr., sold *The J-A*, the *Mercer Island Reporter,* and the *Port Angeles Daily News* to The Persis Corp. of Hawaii. Under the new ownership *The J-A* has turned an even sharper focus on the Eastside, joining forces with KIRO radio to develop a poll of Eastside residents, adding columns devoted to Eastside news makers, running more profiles of Eastside people, and establishing a "News of Record" page. The paper annually places well in the Washington Press Association and Sigma Delta Chi competitions. In 1988 the 28,000-circulation paper was honored by the Bellevue Downtown Association for its contributions to the community. "No other media," said the presenter of the award, "has so comprehensively written about the affairs of Bellevue and the Eastside."

As it has matured, The Journal American *has helped the Eastside develop an identity all its own. Photo by Gary Greene*

It was in the 1980s that Seattle's dailies woke up and realized there was life east of Lake Washington. Both started covering the Eastside more aggressively, and in 1985 the *Times* established an Eastside bureau in Bellevue with 10 employees. Likewise, Seattle's TV stations stepped up their Eastside coverage and one, KIRO, established a 12-person Eastside bureau in Bellevue in April 1988. "The Eastside has become an important part of our news coverage," said Beth Baronsky, a public affairs assistant at the station.

On a more grass roots level, the Eastside is home to a handful of weekly newspapers: the *Northshore Citizen* and *Woodinville Citizen*, both owned by Persis, as well as the *Woodinville Weekly, Northlake News, Issaquah Press, Kirkland Courier,* and *Sammamish Valley News.*

Though most Puget Sound radio stations call Seattle home, Bellevue-based KLSY is a notable exception. The station switched to a soft-rock format in the mid-1980s and has been growing in popularity ever since, particularly with baby-boom listeners.

Libraries

Northwesterners are notoriously heavy readers and the King County Library System's records confirm it. During 1987, 8.4 million items were checked out, meaning 10 items for each individual in the system's service area. The system circulates more items than any library system west of the Mississippi River and north of Los Angeles.

Thirteen of the system's 36 libraries are located on the Eastside. With a yearly circulation of more than 550,000, the Bellevue Public Library is the fifth largest in the county system. Among the library's latest additions are two computer-assisted reference services, which allow the user access to millions of periodical records and article abstracts.

A further sign that the system is committed to the future came in 1988 when the first library bond issue in more than 20 years won approval. Sixty-four percent of the voters in unincorporated King County, Bothell, Bellevue, and North Bend voted "yes." The $67-million bond issue allowed the system to embark on a 12-year plan of building or expanding 18 libraries. New libraries are planned for Bellevue, Woodinville, Juanita, Pine Lake, upper Snoqualmie Valley, and Carnation-Duvall. Expansions are planned for the Redmond and Newport Way branches.

Human Services

Because it is generally an affluent area, the Eastside often suffers from two stereotypes: First, that its people have no "special needs" that social service agencies might meet, and, second, that its people are too busy living "the good life" to care about others. Both perceptions are wrong.

Like all places, the Eastside is home to its pockets of poverty, to the disabled, to children and elderly with special needs. By the year 2000, for example, Bellevue expects a 133 percent increase in low-income families. Fortunately, it has responded

For those who require special care, such as the disabled and the elderly, the progressive, socially responsive Eastside is the place to call home. Photo by Eric Draper

to such needs, as has the Eastside in general. Dozens of organizations and agencies have been founded to provide services for such people. Here's a sample of them:

—The Eastside Resettlement Center in Bellevue serves a growing refugee population of Vietnamese, Cambodian, Laotian, Hmong, Eastern European, and Middle Eastern people. It helps the newcomers adjust to American life, teaching them everything from English to how to fill out a tax form.

—The Eastside Human Services Council serves as a catalyst for social service agencies; among other things, the council holds an annual forum that focuses on the area's changing needs and on how best to meet those needs.

—The Overlake Service League in Bellevue has helped provide necessities to needy Eastside families for longer than any other such organization. It will mark its 80th anniversary in 1991.

—The Bothell-based Multi Service Centers of North and East King County help provide food and housing for the hungry and homeless.

—Merrywood School in Bellevue provides help to disabled children and their families.

—Jewish Family Services in Bellevue offers programs and counseling to strengthen Jewish families.

—Youth Eastside Services in Bellevue provides individual and family counseling, drug and alcohol abuse prevention, treatment services, and employment assistance for disadvantaged youth.

"There has been a remarkable commitment from Kirkland, Redmond and Bellevue to the idea that cities have an interest and responsibility in social services," Peter Berliner, executive director of Youth Eastside Services, told *The Journal American*. "That's very encouraging. It's a topic cities would not even consider eight years ago."

Much of the help has come from volunteers—and much of the financial support has come from the community itself. That's where the second stereotype is shot down. Eastsiders have proven to be generous donators to a variety of needs. One of the more stunning examples comes at the Bellevue Boys and Girls Club, which raises roughly $250,000 each year at its auction. By contrast, Tacoma's and Portland's clubs raise roughly $150,000—combined. Such giving has helped Bellevue's club, with 3,500 members, become one of the largest such clubs in the nation.

Some other sterling examples of donating for worthy causes:

—In June 1988 the March of Dimes raised $60,000 in its "Bid For a Bachelor" night in Bellevue, the first time the event had ever been held on the Eastside. The amount set a national record for events of that kind.

—In July 1988 the Bellevue Breakfast Rotary Club raised $12,000 to fight polio—in only 20 minutes.

—Although the Eastside represents about one-fifth of King County's population, nearly half of the Children's Hospital Guild Association members reside there.

If Eastsiders don't always realize what a giving community they live in, outsiders certainly do. "When I go to a national convention and share what's going on in Bellevue, people are just amazed that we raise that kind of money," said Marc Dosogne, executive director of the Bellevue Boys and Girls Club.

Churches and Synagogues

Washington ranks relatively low in terms of church and synagogue attendance.
And, statistically, the Eastside is not an exception; a Hebert Research survey in
1987 showed only 57 percent of Eastsiders attend at least one worship service per
month. At the same time, however, the region is home to a dedicated group of wor-
shipers whose faith is extremely important to them. More than one-third of Eastsiders attend at least four worship services per month. And, when asked in 1988 how
important religion was to their holiday celebrations, 49 percent said "very important" and 33 percent said "moderately important." As evidence of the commitment
level, one church, Overlake Christian, once raised $1.4 million for a building
project—in a single day.

Some of the largest churches in the state are located on the Eastside. Newcomers realize this fact, when, for instance, they approach Overlake Christian
Church in Kirkland or Westminster Chapel in Bellevue—and find parking atten-
dants guiding them in. Overlake attracts more than 5,000 people to its three Sunday services. Eastside Foursquare, which moved to Bothell in 1989, has a membership of 3,000. Westminster, a nondenominational church in Bellevue founded in
1964, has 1,500 members. Among the other large churches are Cedar Park Assembly
of God in Bothell, and Neighborhood (Assemblies of God), First Presbyterian,
Sacred Heart Catholic Church, St. Louise Catholic Church, and St. Thomas Episco-
pal Church, all of Bellevue.

The ornate Seattle Temple of the Church of Jesus Christ of Latter-day Saints
rises unmistakably in Bellevue's Eastgate area. Temple De Hirsch Sinai serves the Eastside's Jewish population, as do two Mercer Island synagogues—Herzl-Ner Tamid Con-
servative Congregation and Temple B'Nai Torah.

The Eastside has eight Catholic churches and more than 141 Protestant
churches. It is home to Korean churches, Spanish churches, Japanese churches, and
Buddhist temples. In other words, variety reigns. A Hebert Research study showed
the Eastside has 75 denominations. Some people meet with hundreds of fellow wor-
shipers; others with only a handful. Some meet amid the opulence of stained-glass
windows; others in the simplicity of school gymnasiums. Together they weave a pat-
tern of diversity that makes up the fascinating fabric known as the Eastside.

7

OUT AND ABOUT

One August evening Ron Hook of Redmond was piloting his hot-air balloon over a Woodinville neighborhood when a woman below came out of her home.

"Hey," she said, "come on down for a cup of coffee."

"Can't," said Hook. "I've got five people up here."

"Don't worry," she said. "I've got five cups down here."

Hot-air balloons may be the Eastside's quintessential symbol of leisure—people in the air and people on the ground linked by a shared appreciation of the gentle giants. Each summer the balloons gracefully float down the Sammamish Valley, silhouetted against the pinkish orange of a fading sky. In their simplicity they subtly beckon Eastsiders to stop and smell the roses, to forget about bottom lines, to simply relax. And Eastsiders have plenty of opportunities to do just that, whether it be floating along in a hot-air balloon, perusing the latest exhibit at the Bellevue Art Museum, or waterskiing after a day at the office.

Seattle wasn't the birthplace of Recreational Equipment Incorporated (REI) for no reason. Outdoor enthusiasts are so abundant that if Washington had a state fabric it would be Gore-Tex. "One of the reasons we moved here was because of the

Each summer hot-air bal-
loons float gracefully down
the Sammamish Valley. This
balloon is poised over Redmond. Photo by Gary
Greene

to the Eastside. Dance schools, including a branch of the highly respected Pacific Northwest Ballet, had blossomed. And, of more far-reaching effect, plans were being finalized for a performing arts center in downtown Bellevue. The center will include a 500-seat theater. In addition, a smaller center for the performing arts is being proposed for Kirkland. Many see the centers as key cogs in establishing the Eastside as a first-rate home for the arts.

Facing page: Lake Washington, 18 miles long, is a perfect place for Eastside sailors. Photo by Gary Greene

Boating

Everyone loves a parade. But few people ever see the kind of parades that the Eastside and Seattle area are accustomed to: parades on water. Opening day of boating season in this area is a dawn-to-dusk celebration. Boat owners begin to seek good parade-viewing sites up to 24 hours before the parade even begins. The parade, which is held on the Lake Washington Ship Canal in early May, is a celebration of one of Puget Sound's most cherished activities: boating.

On the Eastside, one in four residents owns a boat, according to Hebert Research. The reason is simple: The area is blessed with a myriad of prime places to use them. Newcomers may be awed at the size of Lake Sammamish, which stretches roughly the length of Bellevue to the east. They're even more awed when they realize Lake Washington, 18 miles long, is considerably larger than Lake Sammamish, and that Puget Sound makes Lake Washington look like a duck pond. The San Juan Islands dot Puget Sound like forest-covered jewels, beckoning sailors whose idea of a good time is dropping anchor in a quiet cove and going after some fresh clams and crab for a festive on-board dinner.

Where else in the country can you sail to a college football game? Some Eastsiders do exactly that, mooring outside University of Washington Husky Stadium and taking a dinghy to shore. No tailgate parties for them; just galley parties. At Christmas the Eastside's Christmas parade doesn't go down Main Street; it goes down Lake Washington. Boats lit up with blinking lights and filled with maritime Christmas carolers ring in the holidays. And when the salmon season opens, Eastside boaters can hit Lake Washington and Puget Sound early in the morning, bag their limit, and be at the office in time for that 11 o'clock meeting.

Outdoor Fun

Half an hour from downtown Bellevue, you can be riding a horse in a forest cathedral known as Bridle Trails Park, teeing it up at Bear Creek Country Club, or hiking the Issaquah Alps. In an hour, you can be at the crest of the Cascades or on a ferry to the San Juan Islands. In just over two hours, you can be riding a tandem bike through Stanley Park in Vancouver, British Columbia, or watching Pacific Ocean breakers at Westport. Variety and close proximity are the cornerstones of recreational opportunities available to Eastsiders.

You can tell the seasons on the Eastside by looking at the tops of cars. In winter you'll find skis on those cars. Four snow-skiing areas—Snoqualmie, Ski Acres, Alpental, and Pacific West—are within an hour from the Eastside and offer over 50 downhill runs, cross-country skiing trails, snowboarding, inner-tubing, and night skiing.

In spring, out come the bicycles. Redmond has developed a well-earned reputation as the bicycle capital of the Northwest. Cyclists glide along the Sammamish River Trail and through the farmland of the Snoqualmie Valley to the east. At Marymoor Park, the Northwest's only velodrome plays host to speed cyclists every Friday night in the summer. The city hopes to break ground on a national bicycle museum at the park during the 1990 Goodwill Games, whose bicycle events will be held in Redmond. Already, the city attracts some of the country's finest competitive cyclists; in 1989 the U.S. Track Cycling Championships were held in Redmond.

Meanwhile, with the melting of winter snow, the Cascades beckon the Eastside's hikers, fishermen, campers, and rock climbers. By summer, Eastside cars tend to have sailboards and kayaks attached to their racks. Lake Washington, particularly off Kirkland, has proven a good spot for sailboarders, while kayakers are a short ride away from Cascade Range rivers and—for those who prefer sea kayaking—Puget Sound.

You can tell fall has arrived when the car racks are no longer carrying any-

thing. On the Eastside, people's leisure attention in the autumn tends to shift from participant sports to a particular spectator sport: football.

Spectator Sports

If you want to understand how seriously some Northwesterners take their football, you need to see the converted mail truck that one fan has painted half purple and gold (for University of Washington) and half blue and green (for the Seattle Seahawks). Sellouts at Husky Stadium and the Kingdome are almost foregone conclusions. Football isn't a game in Seattle, it's an event, where most fans arrive early in the morning to start their tailgate parties and hang around long afterward—in most cases, to savor a victory. The Huskies have gone to bowl games 10 of the last 11 years. The Seahawks, meanwhile, have never had a losing season since head coach Chuck Knox arrived in 1983, have made the playoffs four times, and in 1988 won the NFL's American Football Conference Western Division championship.

But football isn't the only game in town. The Seattle Supersonics, National

Football is a popular pastime in Seattle, as sellout crowds at the Kingdome can easily attest. Photo by Gary Greene

Basketball Association champs in 1979, and the Seattle Mariners American League baseball team give the area professional teams in three major sports.

Beyond that, the GTE Northwest Classic golf tournament, featuring the finest senior pro golfers in the world, is held annually at the Eastside's Inglewood Country Club. Golfers such as Jack Nicklaus and Arnold Palmer have teed it up at Redmond's Sahalee Country Club for exhibitions that have drawn thousands. At Marymoor Park the annual Evergreen Classic equestrian event has become prestigious enough to offer $25,000 in prizes and warrant television coverage by ESPN. Longacres racetrack in Renton, just south of Bellevue, attracts those interested in horses for their speed rather than their jumping ability. And, for people who like a little noise with their speed, the annual Seafair hydroplane races on Lake Washington have become as traditional to this area as Thanksgiving football to Detroit, drawing the nation's top boats and drivers.

Places to Go, Things to Do

For those whose idea of a good time is less ambitious than, say, kayaking, opportunities abound nearby. Perhaps the best single area for "poking around" is the Snoqualmie Valley. In the foothills of the Cascades, Snoqualmie Falls—100 feet higher than Niagara—makes a dramatic destination for a Sunday drive. The new Salish Lodge, providing fine dining and rooms with elegant country charm, is perched next to the falls. Nearby, a steam train operated by the Puget Sound Railway Historical Association offers a scenic 10-mile ride that includes views of the falls.

Beyond such offerings, the area boasts the Herbfarm at Fall City, where thousands—yes, thousands—are annually on the lunch waiting list; wine tasting at the Snoqualmie Winery; and a close-up look at Carnation's "contented cows" at the

Facing page: Nature lovers can find pristine wilderness and beautiful mountain peaks within easy driving distance. Photo by Gary Greene

Below: After a scenic half-hour drive from downtown Bellevue, hiking the Issaquah Alps is a healthy and invigorating way to spend an afternoon. Photo by Eric Draper

company's 1,200-acre research farm, complete with picnic facilities.

Across the Eastside, dozens of parks—Bellevue alone has 44—are available for fun-seekers. Lake Sammamish Park, operated by King County, draws more than a million people per year, second only to the Kingdome in terms of visitors. On the opposite end of the lake, the north, Marymoor Park—the largest in the county—is home to the Marymoor Historic Museum, model-airplane fields, ball fields, and expansive picnic grounds. Kelsey Creek Park is a rural oasis in the heart of Bellevue—complete with barns and farmland, a farm-animal viewing area, and pony rides for children.

In the summer Eastsiders can take their choice of fairs and festivals that go on every weekend. The fair season begins in May with the Duvall Days Country Livin' Festival, hits a peak over the Fourth of July when Bothell hosts its popular Freedom Festival and Redmond offers its Heritage Festival, and winds up in early September with Fall City's Harvest Festival.

Whether it's racing sailboats on Lake Washington, listening to jazz at Ste. Michelle Winery, or playing racquetball at the Bellevue Athletic Club, Eastsiders have plenty to do in their leisure time. And plenty to talk about come Monday morning at the office.

EPILOGUE
TOMORROW'S EASTSIDE

I n 1925 Betty Lambert and her father got off the ferry at Medina and started walking east toward what is now downtown. Her father, a Seattle teacher, had accepted a position in Bellevue; it was time to check out the family's new town. By the time they got to a spot near the present-day Security Pacific Plaza, they were puzzled. "We stopped a farmer and asked where we might find Bellevue," said Lambert.

"You just walked through it," he said.

Today, nobody drives across one of the floating bridges and misses Bellevue—or the rest of the Eastside for that matter. What once was only fir trees, strawberry patches, and dirt roads is now a bustling blend of the urban, suburban, and rural. Where that farmer once stood now stands a 25-story high rise. The past and the present make for startling contrasts. And so, too, do the present and the future.

What of Bellevue and the Eastside's future? That question is on the minds of many Eastsiders whose drive and imagination have helped shape this place. People such as Mark Hinshaw, urban designer for the city of Bellevue. "Downtown has so much development potential that it probably won't be filled with capacity until well after 2050," Hinshaw told The Journal American. "By 2010 expect to see at least six new 30- to 40-story high-rise towers downtown."

More immediately, a $27.9-million convention center, approved by the city council in 1989, will be built in the early 1990s. A performing arts center is also on the drawing boards and, when built, will be a major piece in the Eastside's cultural makeup. Other amenities will add luster to downtown's already eye-opening image: the pedestrian corridor, perhaps featuring European-style plazas and cafes; the expansion of the downtown park; more retail stores at street level; more residential high rises such as the Pacific Regent; perhaps an addition to Bellevue Square; and much, much more.

"All in all, Bellevue probably will be a better place to live in than it is now," said Hinshaw. "There'll be more diversity and more interesting things to do. But it will retain its residential charm. It will still be Bellevue."

*Facing page: Snoqualmie
Falls makes a dramatic desti-
nation for a Sunday drive.
The falls are 100 feet higher
than Niagara Falls. Photo by
Eric Draper*

City leaders in Bellevue are pursuing the future with gusto. In 1989 The Bellevue Forum, a series of six public presentations to assess the city's future, was held to help answer the question, "So, where do we go from here?" Inspired by the Frank Lloyd Wright exhibit, the series included national experts such as Neal Peirce, the *Washington Post* columnist and syndicated writer.

In other cities on the Eastside, the future teems with potential. In Redmond the planned Town Center shopping center would give the city its first retail anchor, a focal point that many believe is long overdue. In Issaquah some see the city becoming a mecca for tourists and a home for high-quality office parks. Kirkland's Carillon Point gives the city a classy multiuse development on Lake Washington, yet doesn't infringe on its village-like character. In Bothell a rejuvenated downtown, plus the spin-off benefits of its high-tech neighbors and a University of Washington branch campus scheduled to open in 1990, give the Eastside's north end promise. And to the east, plans such as Weyerhaeuser's Snoqualmie Ridge development, a 30-year project that would include some 3,600 homes, a 350-acre office complex, and a PGA golf course, could bolster sagging rural economies.

By the year 2000 the Eastside's population is expected to nearly double in areas such as Woodinville and East Lake Sammamish. According to projections by the Puget Sound Council of Governments, Bellevue can expect nearly 10,000 more people and the Redmond area 23,000 more. As a whole, the Eastside is expected to have some 450,000 people by the year 2000, according to the Eastside Transportation Program. "Seattle will be a smaller actor on an even more crowded stage," outgoing Seattle mayor Charles Royer told *The Journal American.*

The Eastside's challenge in the future is meeting the same challenge it has been meeting for years—accommodating growth in a controlled fashion that preserves the area's livability. "We must take the action necessary to protect the Northwest way of life for generations to come," King County executive Tim Hill told *Seattle Business* magazine in 1988. "To keep King County from becoming another southern California by the year 2000, government, business and citizens will have to cooperate."

Some favor a stronger regional government to deal with regional problems such as transportation and waste disposal. Others wonder if the time has come for the Eastside to become a county unto its own. Whatever the government structure, the goals are to nurture a thriving economy and meet the needs that thriving economy creates. Traffic, housing, social services, solid waste, recreation—all must be dealt with as the Eastside continues its climb into the twenty-first century.

"I know of no way of judging the future but by the past," Patrick Henry once said. Judging from the Eastside's past, it can meet its future challenges. For this is a region built by people who cared about quality, people who have appreciated the importance of both economy and environment. The Eastside, says Redmond Chamber of Commerce director Dan Ramirez, doesn't need to choose between the two. "We can have it all," he told *The Journal American.*

We can have the best of both worlds: A place with towering trees and towering buildings. A place to work and play. And, yes, a place newcomers can find without having to ask a farmer for directions. As Washington celebrates its centennial, Eastsiders can enthusiastically commemorate the past, proudly celebrate the present, and eagerly consider the future.

PART 2
EASTSIDE ENTERPRISES

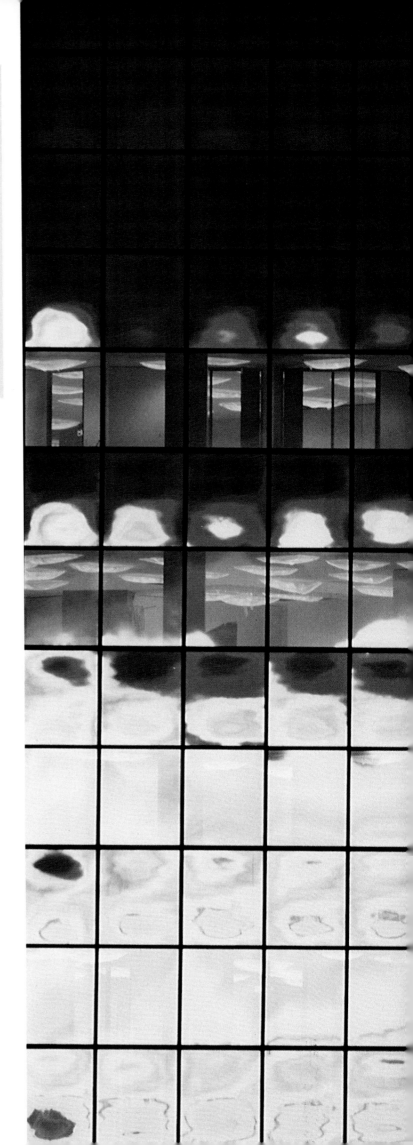

As the city's annual income has increased, spurred by the success of local business, so has the availability of office space. Photo by Wolfgang Kaehler

8 NETWORKS

Bellevue's energy and communication providers keep information and power circulating throughout the Eastside.

Courtesy, IMAGE Productions

The Journal American, 118-121

Puget Sound Power & Light Company, 122-123

Washington Natural Gas, 124

KLSY Radio, 125

Viacom Cable, 126

THE JOURNAL AMERICAN

Facing page: The Journal American's main office building is the nerve center for the Eastside's daily community newspaper; it houses the newsroom, the managerial offices, and the advertising department.

Left: The state-of-the-art Color Printing Center produces 300,000 impressions each week, not including extra commercial jobs.

As the Eastside grows and prospers, it has a partner in its daily community newspaper—*The Journal American.*

Since becoming a daily newspaper in 1976, the JA has grown in circulation and revenue, and has helped establish the identity of the Eastside.

"We're unabashed supporters of the Eastside community," says Robert J. Weil, the 39-year-old publisher. "As this community grows, we want to help shape its agenda to ensure the quality of life that attracts so many people."

With a daily circulation approaching 30,000, the paper has effectively gained an audience that reads the JA for one reason: It is the only source of comprehensive news, comment, and opinion about the Eastside. But getting there hasn't been easy.

Looking back at the early years of the paper, Weil observes: "There used to be a time when many residents viewed Bellevue and the Eastside as an extension of Seattle. We were bedroom communities serving the needs of Seattle commuters. But that trend has changed dramatically in recent years. Now the Eastside is forging ahead with is own distinct identity."

Making the JA more local by providing in-depth and exclusive coverage of Bellevue and the Eastside came with the paper's change in ownership. In March 1986 the Hawaii-based Persis Corp. purchased the paper. Chairman Thurston Twigg-Smith, long respected for his leadership as a champion of community service and excellence at the *Honolulu Advertiser,* made clear his commitment to a strong tradition of community journalism.

The Journal American is building on that tradition, starting with the legacy of its two weekly predecessors and integrating it with the sophisticated, fast-paced world of the contemporary Eastside. *The Journal American* intends to be the primary source of news and advertising for the communities it serves.

Persis established Northwest Media Inc., a wholly owned subsidiary headquartered in Bellevue. Weil is president in Northwest Media Inc., which publishes *The Journal American,* the *Peninsula Daily News* in Port Angeles, and two weeklies, the *Mercer Island Reporter* and the *Citizen* of Bothell and Woodinville.

Persis also publishes the *Honolulu Advertiser* and the *Knoxville News Journal,* and is involved in real estate as well. In all its

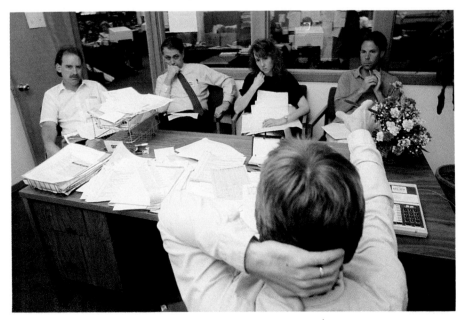

Editor John S. Perry discusses the next day's page one lineup with director of photography Jeff Larsen, city editor Jack Mayne, copy editor Laurie Bruscas, and assistant city editor Tim Talevich.

At an editorial board meeting are (from left to right): editorial page editor Karl Thunemann, editorial writer Craig Groshart, publisher Robert Weil, and editor John S. Perry.

operations, the firm employs some 470 people and reports assets totaling $120 million.

Beyond the company's aggressive commitment to community service, employees of the JA have an added incentive to be productive and creative. Employees own 30 percent of the firm and are actually partners with the Twigg-Smith family. The company's employee stock ownership plan has helped the paper recruit new talent.

"Community journalism is our greatest strength," says Weil, a 13-year veteran of the Gannett/ *USA Today* group. "We are always looking for ways to intensify our focus and make the JA an indispensable reading habit of Eastside residents."

Within months after arriving as publisher, Weil initiated changes in the paper's format and internal management structure. In an effort to become the primary source of news and advertising for the Eastside, the newspaper's reporters and editors began paying closer attention to Eastside people and issues.

The paper was redesigned and reorganized, allowing quick access to the day's news. It aims to be the Eastside's newspaper of record—from providing a calendar of each day's public meetings, to telling what the police and courts did, to providing information about the key issues facing the Eastside in the coming decade.

To better define the newspaper's personality, editor John S. Perry created several new positions, including a regional issues reporter and the paper's first full-time columnist, while committing the paper to in-depth reporting on issues such as affordable housing on the Eastside.

Perry's intention is to establish the paper as the agenda-setter of the entire community. Such issues as traffic and mass transportation, growth, water supply and quality, and public safety would receive critical attention.

The 38-year-old editor also worked to expand business coverage and include accounts of the Eastside's growing social scene in the "Living" section.

Today the paper is an influential source of news and views, and is delivering on its promise to be the voice of the Eastside.

The Journal American's efforts to refine its coverage have not gone unnoticed. The front wall of the cluttered newsroom displays many plaques citing editorial excellence. Awards from the Washing-

Reviewing a news story on the computer are (from left): editor John S. Perry, city editor Jack Mayne, and publisher Robert Weil.

Publisher Robert Weil peruses the day's newspaper before a roomful of giant news-print rolls.

ton Press Association and the Society of Professional Journalists, to name a few, recognize the paper for excellence in business, sports, and news coverage, as well as for individual writing, editing, and design. The JA's sports section regularly has been ranked among the top 10 nationally for its circulation by The Associated Press.

Under Weil's guidance, the challenge of selling advertising space has been met with a modern marketing effort aimed at major retailers who recognize the higher-than-average median incomes of Eastside residents and the buying power of the community as a whole.

National advertisers, meanwhile, are becoming more aware of the paper's upscale and mobile demographics.

Weil and his staff believe there's much to do as the JA grows, yet a solid foundation has been set.

The Journal American's efforts of recent years have been part of a larger strategy to position the

paper for the future. If economic predictions are realized, the population of the Eastside will well exceed that of Seattle within a few years. *The Journal American* aspires to become the Eastside's premier

news source. In 13 short years it already has come a long way toward providing the best in local news coverage. Its goal is to become a standard by which others are measured.

Before going to press, pages are pasted up in The Journal American*'s composing room.*

ROOTS OF A NEWSPAPER

The Journal American began publishing in 1976 when Longview Publishing Company, a regional, family-owned publishing company, purchased and combined the editorial efforts of two local weekly papers, the *East Side Journal* and the *Bellevue American.*

The two community weeklies had been published by family-owned businesses since 1918 and 1930, respectively. As publisher, John McClelland, Jr., saw the potential for making the paper a daily and set out to build a local advertising and subscriber base.

McClelland, a longtime member of the Associated Press Board of Governors and a state historian, brought a lifelong commitment to quality journalism to the task. His personal sense of the Northwest is reflected in the sylvan setting of *The Journal American*'s offices on 132nd Avenue NE. The newspaper occupied the building in 1978. At 20,000 square feet, it cost $4 million.

In August 1984 the JA opened the Color Printing Center next door to the paper's offices. The center has state-of-the-art presses and a computerized mailroom providing the JA and its companion publications the best color reproduction in the Puget Sound area. In addition, the Color Printing Center handles a large volume of commercial printing.

In 1985 diverging objectives among the company's owners led them to put *The Journal American* up for sale. In November of that year McClelland announced that company—including the JA—was being sold to the Persis Corp.

PUGET SOUND POWER & LIGHT COMPANY

Puget Sound Power & Light Company serves the fastest-growing counties in the Pacific Northwest, providing electric power for some 1.5 million people in western Washington. Headquartered in Bellevue, Puget Power is one of the Eastside's largest employers, with 2,500 workers.

The company is the descendant of Seattle Electric Light Company, which began providing electricity to Puget Sound residents more than a century ago. Now the largest investor-owned electric utility in the state, Puget Power provides electricity to a 4,500-square-mile service area that includes eight counties bordering Puget Sound in western Washington and part of Kittitas County in central Washington, just east of the Cascade Mountain Range.

By 1912 more than 50 local firms consolidated under the name Puget Sound Traction, Light & Power Company. The name was changed to Puget Sound Power & Light Company in 1920, following the sale of several transportation properties. By 1924 the firm furnished virtually all the electric railway service in the Puget Sound district.

In the 1930s, after building a number of smaller dams in western Washington, the company took a giant step, constructing Rock Island Dam, the first ever to span the Columbia River. The organization was forced to sell Rock Island Dam and lost nearly one-half of its service area and many of its facilities to municipal and PUD systems between 1937 and 1952, a time of high momentum for the public power movement.

In 1959 Puget Power completed its Baker River Develop-

Dispatchers at Puget Power's Eastside System Operations Center in Redmond use state-of-the-art technology to control the company's transmission and generation network.

Left: Puget Power's linemen work day and night to provide a steady flow of electricity to about 1.5 million people within the company's 4,500-square-mile service area.

Below: Participants in Puget Power's nationally recognized Consumer Panels program are shown touring a power production plant. The Consumer Panels serve as a forum for the exchange of ideas between the utility's management and its customers. More than 1,000 recommendations presented by the Consumer Panels have been implemented into Puget Power's planning process.

ment, adding the Upper Baker River Dam and powerhouse to the existing Lower Baker facilities. Between 1971 and 1985 Puget Power joined other utilities in building the four-phase Colstrip plant in southeastern Montana, the largest capital investment in the company's history. Work on the two original 330-megawatt Colstrip coal-fired power plants began in the fall of 1971; commercial operation began in 1975 and 1976.

In late 1956 Puget Power opened and began operating from Bellevue's first "skyscraper," the four-story General Office Building. Today the company occupies that building as well as nine floors of neighboring One Bellevue Center. Puget Power has offices on the Eastside in Bellevue, Redmond, Kirk-

land, Bothell, and Snoqualmie, as well as in communities throughout its service territory.

The nerve center of its power system, the Eastside System Operations Center, is in Redmond, where, since 1985, a sophisticated Energy Management System (EMS) places the entire transmission and generation network under the central control of the power dispatchers and system operators.

Puget Power's service territory is one of the fastest growing areas in the nation. During the past 10 years the company has added 209,000 new customers. In 1988 alone, more than 23,000 customer hookups were recorded. If state population forecasts are realized, one-half of the nearly 500,000 new residents expected by the year 2000 will settle somewhere in Puget Power's service area.

Puget Power owns Snoqualmie Falls, one of the state's most popular scenic attractions. It draws more than 800,000 visitors per year and is the site of the first major electric plant in the Northwest to use falling water as a power source. The Snoqualmie Falls project was an intricate undertaking, patterned after Niagara Falls. Completed in 1899, it is still producing power for today's consumers. Through the years the firm has maintained the beauty of the land surrounding the falls. Perched on the overlook to the

Snoqualmie Falls attracts more than 800,000 visitors annually and is the site of the first major hydroelectric plant in the Pacific Northwest to use falling water as a power source. The plant was constructed nearly a century ago. At left is Salish Lodge, offering visitors dining, scenic views, and overnight accommodations.

falls is the Salish Lodge, featuring resort accommodations and fine dining. The Salish Lodge and Country Cafe are owned by Puget Western, a subsidiary of Puget Power, and operated by the Oregon-based Salishan Lodge.

Puget Power is involved in the communities it serves, listening to its customers through its nationally recognized Consumer Panel program. Consumer Panel recommendations have helped Puget Power develop ways to improve customer service, make critical long-range power supply decisions, take maximum advantage of conservation as an energy resource, find new ways to meet the needs of at-risk sectors of its customer population, and take a leading role in the economic development of the communities it serves.

One of the at-risk groups most dramatically served by Puget Power is the growing percentage of aging people, many of whom are too proud to seek assistance directly from public agencies. The nationally acclaimed Gatekeeper Program was developed to train utility employees to look out for and help older customers, and to refer them to sources of assistance.

Nearly 90 private electric utilities have adopted the Gatekeeper Program, and in December 1988 the American Association of Retired Persons honored Puget Power with its highest national award. In addition, the company has received the President's Citation for the Gatekeeper Program as well as other national awards and recognition for its innovative elderly services.

Puget Power received the 1988 Edison Electric Award for its service programs. The coveted award is conferred annually on the one electric utility that best serves as a model for the industry.

Puget Power is active on the local economic development front. Since 1988 it has sponsored a series of day-long forums called Economic Summits. Serving as a catalyst, the company has brought together community leaders to assess the area's problems and challenges. Among the positive results has been the commitment of more than $30 million of new investment and the promise of 700 new jobs.

The company also supports major community projects. Puget Power chairman John Ellis headed up the private-sector effort to develop Bellevue Downtown Park. The company itself sponsors the Challenge Series, an annual soapbox-style race event for handicapped children in communities throughout the Puget Sound area, including the Eastside. Corporate contributions and company volunteers support many more public service efforts.

Puget Power has made a major commitment to conservation, investing some $185 million in energy-saving programs. The action plan includes such resource-conserving choices as weatherization and use of energy-efficient water heaters and appliances.

Looking ahead, Puget Power pledges to seek new ways to offer reliable, high-quality customer service at a competitive price.

WASHINGTON NATURAL GAS

Washington Natural Gas began operating in 1873 as Seattle Gas Light Company, serving only a handful of customers and primarily supplying street lighting. The firm's first plant produced gas from coal and piped it through the city in bored-out fir logs.

Today the company serves more than 328,000 commercial, industrial, and residential customers in five counties—King, Pierce, Lewis, Snohomish, and Thurston. Washington Natural Gas provides more energy each year than any other utility in the state.

Since its introduction, gas has become increasingly popular for space heating, water heating, clothes drying, and cooking in the home. Natural gas also is used in industry because it is among the most easily controlled sources of energy. Industries throughout the area use gas for everything from firing furnaces and kilns to forging, cutting, hardening, drying, purifying, fabricating, processing, curling, and shaping materials.

Natural gas replaced manufactured gas in 1956. Natural gas flows into the state through major pipelines linking Puget Sound customers with the gas fields in the

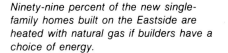

Ninety-nine percent of the new single-family homes built on the Eastside are heated with natural gas if builders have a choice of energy.

American Southwest and Canada.

That same year the company's gas lines extended to the east side of Lake Washington, serving Seattle's bedroom communities. Because these communities were thriving with activity, the company established an Eastern Division in 1961 to serve residents and businesses in the area more efficiently. The Eastern Division office was opened at 156th Avenue N.E. and N.E. Eighth Street in Bellevue (across from Crossroads Mall), where it currently is located. When the office opened, the company was serving some 6,200 Eastside customers. Today Washington Natural Gas serves more than 84,000 commercial, industrial, and residential customers on the Eastside.

With the rate of growth increasing, the Eastside is creating some bedroom communities of its own, including North Bend and Du-

The Washington Natural Gas Eastern Division office serves more than 84,000 residential, commercial, and industrial customers on the Eastside.

vall. The largest surge is in housing construction. Washington Natural Gas is rapidly extending its gas lines in response to these growing communities' requests for gas service.

Throughout the area the use of natural gas in single-family homes has flourished. More than 40 percent of the existing single-family homes are heated with natural gas. Builders of 99 percent of the new single-family homes on the Eastside insist on installing natural gas heating equipment where they have a choice of energy.

While business for home builders is thriving, builders of office buildings and retail space also are contributing to the growth. Office parks and retail strip malls continue to emerge along the I-90 and I-405 corridors, especially between Bellevue and Bothell. More architects, builders, owners, and developers are requesting natural gas in these new buildings.

Washington Natural Gas is a subsidiary of Washington Energy Company, which has operations in 13 states and three Canadian provinces. The parent company's interests include distribution of natural gas, marketing of energy and conservation services and products, coal holdings, and oil and gas exploration and development.

KLSY RADIO

KLSY-FM is a radio station that listens to its listeners. From the day in July 1983 when it signed on the air with new call letters and a new format, the Bellevue station has based its programming on listener input and has carved a niche in a fickle marketplace.

In the early 1960s the station signed on as KZAM, known for its rock-and-roll format. In June 1966 the station was purchased by F. Kemper Freeman and its call letters changed to KFKF-FM. It was sold to A. Stewart Ballinger in 1972 and became KBES-FM. Late in 1974 it became KZAM-FM again.

Dudley White, owner and operator of Sandusky Newspapers, Inc., bought the station in 1978, the first radio acquisition by the company. Sandusky has since acquired stations in San Diego, Denver, Kansas City, Dallas, Tampa, and Phoenix.

KZAM-FM became a well-known area rock station. But in 1983 the station management made the risky decision to change the successful format and identity. The decision has not been regretted. The change was based on evidence that there was a hole in the FM adult-contemporary market. Studies indicated the rock format offered limited growth, owing to intense competition and an aging audience. Management decided to pursue a more sophisticated listener whose buying power would attract upscale advertisers.

Listeners immediately noticed KLSY's difference—hit-oriented music with notably softer sounds and less repetition. The programming featured music from the 1970s and 1980s with a sprinkling

of oldies and new music. The station signed on with nothing but music for the first few weeks; listeners were asked to call in requests. The traditional elements were gradually added back, including Bruce Murdock's popular morning show.

The "Lights Out" program begins nightly at 7 p.m., featuring

Bruce Murdock has developed a morning rapport with KLSY's adult-contemporary audience.

soft, romantic tunes.

Issues such as the school system, traffic, and drug abuse are important to the KLSY audience; the news department keeps on its toes to cover these stories.

The nationally acclaimed Teddy Bear Patrol, launched by KLSY in 1987, is among the most successful radio promotions in the country. The idea evolved from a program undertaken by the Boulder, Colorado, Police Department, where policemen carried new teddy bears in the trunks of their patrol cars to help ease situations in which children were involved.

KLSY asked listeners to help supply the Bellevue and Seattle police departments with 1,000 bears to be given to children in traumatic situations. Response was

overwhelming. The first test came when a two-year-old child was lured from a window ledge, agreeing to come down if she could have the bear.

Since then police departments throughout the Puget Sound have been "armed" with new teddy bears in the trunks of their patrol cars—all supplied by KLSY listeners. The bears have been used to comfort children in situations ranging from child abuse to rape. The Teddy Bear Patrol reaches some 71 law enforcement agencies in Kitsap, Pierce, Snohomish, and King counties. In 1988 more than 10,000 bears were collected, and KLSY garnered coverage by *Newsweek* magazine.

KLSY has associated itself with hundreds of other causes, including the Christmastime Giving Tree program and an annual live New Year's Eve broadcast from the Space Needle, dubbed the "Times Square of the West."

The station recently moved its antenna to West Tiger Mountain, more than 3,000 feet above sea level. KLSY's signal now is one of the best in the area. The $500,000 investment involved the purchase of a state-of-the-art antenna that concentrates the broadcast signal on the desired coverage area while minimizing reflections from the mountains, the first in the Puget Sound region.

KLSY management is constantly defining its audience and assessing its tastes and needs. The station is planning more community involvement and upgraded signal strength. KLSY management is keenly aware of the bottom line in radio success—listener loyalty.

VIACOM CABLEVISION

The cable television industry emerged in the late 1940s as a response to viewers' desires for better TV reception. One of the oldest and fastest growing cabled areas in the country is the Puget Sound region, much of which is served by Viacom Cablevision.

While clear reception was the original selling point of cable service, today's cable TV offers the advantage of programming variety and selection. Viacom's lineup offers children's programming, news, sports, finance, classic movies, comedy, dance, and theater—something for everyone.

Viacom has run more than 2,589 miles of cable throughout the region and has invested millions of dollars to assure customers receive the best cable television has to offer—both in entertainment and in technology. The company's vision clearly states that: "The mission of Viacom Cablevision is to provide quality entertainment with excellent customer service and to fulfill our responsibilities to the community."

Recognizing that customer satisfaction is the most important as-

Viacom's maintenance technicians regularly inspect and test aerial cable equipment.

pect of the industry, Viacom stresses efficiency and convenience. Offices are open evenings, Saturdays, and holidays. There are extended hours for its phone lines and a 24-hour service line. Service calls receive same-day or next-day response.

Viacom also puts a high priority on community service activities. On any given weekend, as

many as 50 of Viacom's employees are involved in various projects, ranging from neighborhood cleanups to fund-raising events for groups such as Big Brothers and Big Sisters, Children's Hospital, the Boys and Girls Clubs, or the Children's Home Society.

In an effort to recognize community spirit in others, the Viacom Community Service Scholarship was established in 1987. It is awarded annually to a Bellevue public high school senior in recognition of volunteer work and can be used for continuing education at the institution of the student's choice.

Viacom Cablevision of Puget Sound was originally made up of a group of small cable systems owned by private investors. In 1965 Tele-Vue Systems, Inc., purchased the cable systems, and in 1971 Tele-Vue Systems became Viacom Cablevision.

Viacom's parent company, New York-based Viacom International, Inc., is a diversified entertainment communications company engaged in television, radio, and feature film ventures. Viacom International and its subsidiaries employ some 4,700 people worldwide.

Viacom Cablevision's regional office in Everett. Offices are also located in Redmond, Seattle, Tacoma, Monroe, Oak Harbor, Federal Way, Puyallup, Lakewood, and Fort Lewis.

Photo by Gary Greene

9
INDUSTRY AND HIGH TECHNOLOGY

The Eastside's location and qualified work force draw manufacturers and high-tech industries to the area.

Photo by Jack McConnell. Courtesy, McConnell McNamara & Company

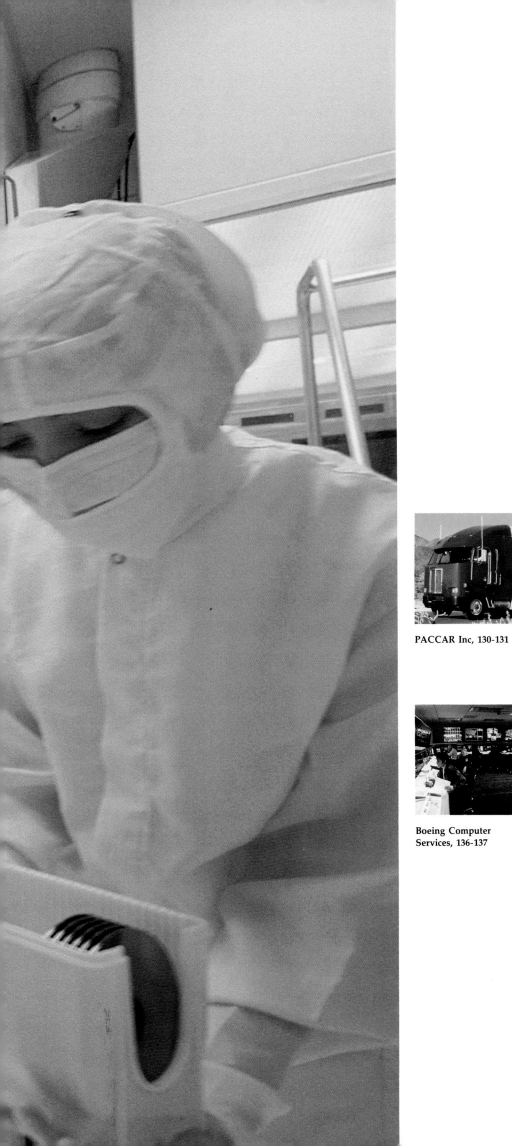

PACCAR INC

One of the largest companies in the Pacific Northwest, PACCAR Inc has experienced extraordinary growth in the past two years. Annual sales and net income in 1988 surpassed all previous records of the 84-year-old multinational company that manufactures heavy-duty on- and off-road Class 8 trucks sold worldwide under the Kenworth, Peterbilt, and Foden nameplates. PACCAR competes in the North American Class 6 and 7 markets with its Mid-Ranger models built to company specifications and sold in North America under the Kenworth and Peterbilt nameplates.

PACCAR also manufactures and markets industrial winches, mining equipment, and oil pumping and extraction pumps. The firm participates in the truck parts aftermarket and sells general auto-

motive parts and accessories through retail and wholesale outlets. Finance and leasing subsidiaries facilitate the sale of PACCAR products in the United States, Canada, Mexico, the United Kingdom, and Australia.

In 1988 PACCAR reported worldwide sales of $3.1 billion, a 28-percent increase over 1987. Employing approximately 14,000 people worldwide, the company operates seven parts distribution centers in North America and 16 factories in four countries. Approximately 3,000 PACCAR employees live

Above: The "connected truck" was introduced by Seattle Car Manufacturing Company, a PACCAR predecessor, in 1909 for transporting logs.

Below: Acquired by PACCAR in 1987, Al's Auto Supply is a leading wholesale and retail distributor of automotive parts and accessories, with more than 29 locations throughout Washington.

in Washington State, and about 1,800 work on the Eastside. PACCAR's corporate headquarters is located in the Business Center Building in downtown Bellevue.

"PACCAR takes pride in being a part of the Eastside community," says Charles M. Pigott, chairman and chief executive officer. "As the area has grown through the years, so has our company. The quality of life enjoyed here enhances both the business environment and the personal lives of our employees."

PACCAR's heritage dates back to 1905, when William Pigott founded the Seattle Car Manufacturing Company in Hubbard, now

Above: A Kenworth T600A negotiates a winding mountain road. The Kenworth Truck Company is one of PACCAR's many subsidiaries.

Left: The sleek Peterbilt 372 is designed for powerful and efficient transport. The Peterbilt Motors Company became part of the PACCAR family in 1958.

part of West Seattle. There, Seattle Car produced four-wheeled cars used by railroads to transport logs for the burgeoning timber industry. In 1908 the firm relocated to a new plant site in Renton. By 1917 Seattle Car merged with the Twohy Brothers Company of Portland, forming the Pacific Car & Foundry Company. The new firm, with plants in both Portland and Renton, achieved immediate success with a government order for 2,000 boxcars needed to move freight during World War I.

In 1924 Pigott sold the firm to pursue other interests in the steel business. During the 1920s, under new ownership, Pacific Car & Foundry diversified into the manufacture of buses, structural-steel fabrications, and metal technology. Spurred by both the promise of new products and his deep pride in the company's history, Paul Pigott, William's son, repurchased Pacific Car & Foundry in 1934.

During World War II Pacific Car built Sherman tanks and wing spars for American bombers. As the peacetime market for trucks increased, the firm acquired Kenworth Truck Company in 1945 and Peterbilt Motors Company in 1958. Charles M. Pigott, Paul's son, was elected president of the corporation in 1965, and seven years later the company was consolidated and renamed PACCAR Inc. In the early 1970s PACCAR purchased Wagner Mining Equipment Co. During the 1980s PACCAR acquired Foden Trucks and Trico Industries, Inc.—an oil pumping and extraction equipment company. The firm also diversified into the general automotive parts and accessories market through its acquisition of more than 130 Grand Auto and Al's Auto Supply stores located in California, Nevada, Washington, and Alaska.

PACCAR Inc maintains exceptionally high standards of quality for all its products, which are well engineered, highly customized for particular applications, and priced to sell in the premium segment of their market, where they have a reputation for innovation, superior performance, and pride of ownership.

PENWEST

Penwest is most likely one of the Northwest's most talked about, most written about, and most closely scrutinized corporations. Why? Because in its five-year history, the company has been involved in a rash of activity that has included Dutch auction stock repurchases, acquisitions, new products, and the sale of one of its divisions, which represented half of its holdings. All of this aggression in the marketplace is based on the firm's mission statement to "create the maximum rate of value growth through long-term profit on invested capital and the growth of that capital by becoming a leading, worldwide producer of high-margin natural and synthetic polymer-based, specialty chemicals and food ingredients."

Bellevue-based Penwest was created in 1984 from a spin-off that brought together two grain-processing subsidiaries of Seattle-based Univar Corp. A high-risk

Penwest is a leader in the research and development of new and sometimes exotic chemical products for the paper industry.

venture, the corporation was comprised of two primary businesses: Great Western Malting Co., which makes malt for brewers, and Penford Products Co., which makes specialty chemical starches for the paper industries.

Led by energetic, young chief executive officer Tod Hamachek, Penwest is a rapidly growing producer of high, value-added specialty carbohydrate and synthetic polymer chemicals, food and flavor ingredients, and agricultural nutrition supplements. The company's principal source of revenue is specialty chemical starch products for the paper and textile industries.

Penwest sold its malting division, Great Western Malting Co., in March 1989 to Canada Malting Co. of Toronto, Canada. Great Western Malting Co. is the leading producer of high-quality brewers' malt in the West, serving brewers throughout the western and southwestern United States and selected nations of the Pacific Rim. The gain from the sale of the division (which accounted for more than half of Penwest's 1988 sales

Penwest's specialty starch chemicals, used in fine writing paper, impart internal strength (bonding), coating, and sizing, which renders paper impervious to fluids such as ink.

of $142 million) was more than $20 million. The money from the sale and some borrowings will be used to finance the expansion of Penford Products and to acquire new companies.

Hamachek's strategy is to downsize the company in order to grow in the long term. Part of a five-year plan, the sale of Great Western Malting Co. reflects the effort to shed lower-yielding assets in slow-growth industries.

Penford Products Co., a division of Penwest, is a leading producer of chemically modified specialty starches and is the paper industry's major supplier of chemical starch coatings. The division's plants are in Cedar Rapids, Iowa, and Idaho Falls, Idaho.

Penford accounted for about 40 percent of the total sales for Penwest in 1988, but an estimated 60 to 65 percent of its profits. The company has a broad customer base and has potential for growth in related fields. In addition, the firm has shown a high rate of return on research and development efforts.

The division's basic business is serving the paper industry, especially the producers of coated and uncoated free sheet papers. Penford produces chemically modified

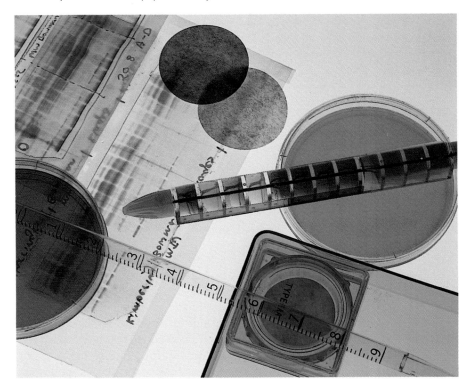

Papers made with Penwest products allow a high degree of color holdout, imparting brilliance and accuracy.

starches used for the coating of high-grade paper such as that used in books, catalogs, and magazines. The company is involved in an intense effort to create new patentable paper chemicals in selected paper industry market niches.

Penford introduced three new products in 1987. Fast Break™ is a plant nutritional supplement that will be used by mushroom growers to speed up their harvest and increase crop yield. The product is based on a modification of a corn wet-milling by-product and is targeted for a $25-million market in the United States and Europe.

Soludex™ is a maltodextrin-based bulking agent used for coffee whiteners, bouillon cubes, powdered drink mixes, and artificial sweeteners. Penford has a 15-percent share of the $40-million market with a similar product.

Quick Wash™ is a specialty modified starch sold to the textile industry to size cloth and yarn during manufacturing, providing a pre-washed feeling to fabrics such as denim. As many as five new products are under development, and six to eight are being considered. Penford will play a pivotal role in

Penwest's strategic goals.

In addition, the company produces food ingredients, an area that has been targeted for expansion. Acquisitions may add other lines, including specialty chemical

products to be sold to the paper and textile industries, plus industrial coatings and adhesives lines.

Hamachek told shareholders at the 1988 annual meeting that he sees for Penford Products exceptionally strong upside potential for the near term with relatively little downside risk. Before it divested itself of Great Western Malting, Penwest employed about 520 people and reported net profits exceeding $9 million, representing a 35-percent return on shareholders' equity.

"We believe that value growth is growth with substance, not with mirrors," Hamachek says. "We believe that long-term value growth comes from the basics in business: intelligent planning, prudent investment of resources, hard work, and aggressive execution. We are in the business for the long term, not just quarter to quarter."

Penwest provides leading paper makers with products and services that improve not only the quality of the paper but the efficiency of production.

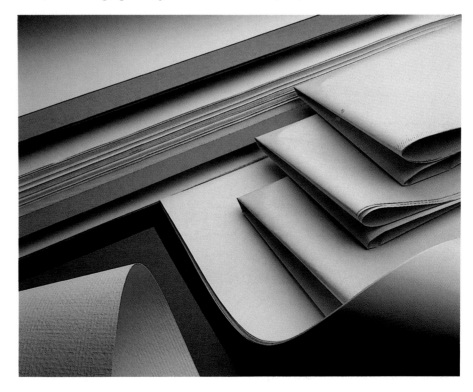

ACCOUNTANTS MICROSYSTEMS, INC.

From its Bellevue headquarters AMI serves an increasing client base of national businesses.

Accountants Microsystems, Inc., is the leading innovator of software that focuses on the accounting marketplace. The company's clients range from small, one-person CPA firms to the largest international accounting firms and *Fortune* 1,000 companies. More than 7,000 firms use AMI software, representing more than 30,000 modules in all.

Since it was founded in 1981, AMI has experienced tremendous growth and change, going from a two-person enterprise in a garage shop to more than 100 employees. It all began in the early 1980s with the advent of the IBM Personal Computer. Two local computer professionals pooled their talents and developed a computer program for accountants called DATAWRITE®. The two entrepreneurs pioneered vertical market microcomputer software for practicing accountants.

Today AMI sells a family of accounting software, including an enhanced version of its original

DATAWRITE® program that helps accountants design charts of accounts, journal formats, and advanced management reports. AMI has also developed other software pertinent to the accounting profession, including the Tax Machine®, a fully integrated in-house system for preparing both individual and business federal and state income tax returns; Managing Partner, a timekeeping, billing, and receivables package that provides the information needed to increase profitability of clients' firms; The Business Partner Series, a general accounting software for clients' use and fully compatible with Datawrite; and Fixed Asset Management, a sophisticated package that monitors and plans depreciation of capital equipment and maintains book, federal, and state deprecia-

tion for each asset. AMI's programmers constantly study current tax law, enhancing and revising the software as needed to reflect the changes.

AMI has grown from a two-person start-up company to a nationally known vendor of premium accounting software. In 1985 the firm recruited outside senior management to help manage its phenomenal growth rate. Originally, AMI sold its software as a part of a turnkey system, with hardware and software packages. The PC had revolutionized office automation, and AMI became an

IBM-PC hardware distributor as well as a software distributor. By 1986 the challenges of selling hardware in addition to software became a drain. Less-expensive clones were selling as well or better than IBM products, and AMI's new management decided to withdraw from the hardware business and design the software so that it could be utilized by a number of different systems, thus making it compatible with many different brands of computers and freeing the company to further develop the family of software it now distributes.

AMI products are made available through a nationwide dealer network that distributes AMI software, helping the company achieve a larger market share and greater growth. AMI is the only organization of its kind to use independent, value-adding representatives as its sole channel of distribution. This method benefits the customer by providing a quality of service that cannot be achieved with other software products.

Local AMI representatives and independent businesses representing AMI give person-to-person attention. This national network of distribution lets AMI concentrate

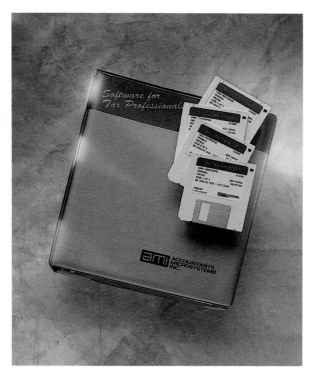

Above: Accountants Microsystems produces software uniquely tailored to the changing needs of today's tax professionals.

Left: The Tax Machine® is AMI's innovative software package that allows individual and business users to compute their state and federal income tax returns.

on what it does best—creating and enhancing premium software products for professional accountants.

Local distributors offer support from the outset, assisting in installation and start-up. For ongoing support, clients may choose plans offered directly from AMI's staff of experts in computers and accounting. AMI's Education Department offers hands-on product training and intensive seminars nationwide and year round. AMI employs district managers nationwide to establish and retain a strong dealer network. AMI products are presently being sold in all 50 states.

In January 1988 Accountant Microsystems was acquired by SCS/Compute, Inc., a St. Louis-based company primarily involved in tax return processing for the accounting profession. Together AMI and SCS provide software and services to more than 10,000 accounting and tax practices.

AMI was conceived in Bellevue, and its management is committed to its headquarters location. The location became even more important in 1988, when AMI needed to hire dozens of software programmers and data-processing experts. The area provided

a pool of high-tech and computer talent.

In addition, the company owes its success to a strong local network of venture capitalists who believed in the technology and its application. The firm has grown as much as 300 percent per year since it was founded, and achieved profitability in its fiscal year ending April 1988. The success of AMI's Tax Machine® for businesses and individuals helped the company increase its profits by 250 percent in its 1989 fiscal year. Today AMI is well positioned to retain and strengthen its position as the leader in the industry.

A 1988 article in *Microsoft Quarterly,* a respected computer magazine, stated, "Even in the microcomputer industry, where rapid-success stories have become commonplace, Accountants Microsystems, Inc., stands out as a company that did everything right."

BOEING COMPUTER SERVICES

Boeing Computer Services, the computing arm of The Boeing Company, supplies computing resources and information services to Boeing operating divisions and to government and commercial customers worldwide.

Operating one of the largest privately owned telecommunications networks in the world, Boeing Computer Services currently occupies 2.7 million square feet of office and computing space from six major data centers, 10 network control centers, and sales offices in cities in the United States, Canada, and Europe.

Boeing Computer Services data centers are located in Bellevue and Kent, Washington; Vienna, Virginia; Wichita, Kansas; Huntsville, Alabama; and Philadelphia, Pennsylvania. Six network control centers are located with the data centers. The other four are in Seattle, Everett, and Renton.

The processing power of the division's IBM mainframe computers is approximately 756 million instructions per second. The division operates significant numbers of IBM and CDC mainframe computers, as well as computing equipment from more than 30 other manufacturers and sources. Equipment inventory, valued at more than one billion dollars, ranges from desk-top personal computers,

Situated in Bellevue amid 92 acres of extensively landscaped and forested grounds, the aesthetically designed 200,000-square-foot Boeing Computer Services data center designs, integrates, manages, and maintains computer systems essential to The Boeing Company's operation.

through a variety of micros, minis, and mainframes, on up to large-scale computers and supercomputers.

Boeing Computer Services was established in May 1970 to consolidate 13 computing organizations within The Boeing Company. The division began with some $250 million of computing equipment and a staff of 2,700.

Today, under the direction of president Michael R. Hallman, the division employs more than 11,000 globally and serves more than 1,500 commercial and government customers with a broad range of systems integration services.

Boeing Computer Services is headquartered in Bellevue on a 90-acre wooded site near I-90 that was opened in 1981. It consists of a 200,000-square-foot data center plus six office buildings, totaling 500,000 square feet.

The division is responsible for designing, integrating, managing, and maintaining a variety of computer systems essential to The Boeing Company's operations. It

has designed interactive databases that increase competitiveness. The division has played a major role in implementing computer-aided design and computer-aided manufacturing (CAD/CAM), including the use of supercomputers to simulate airflow around airplanes.

Boeing Computer Services is a leader in managing and developing complex, integrated information systems. The division provides custom-designed, computer-based information and communication systems, and is one of the largest providers of teleprocessing and computer services to the federal government. It supports federal and state governments by providing systems, including computer hardware and software resources, telecommunications activities, application and support software, and skilled labor. This ranges from designing small Local Area Networks (LANS) and developing software applications to managing large turnkey data communications networks and total computer facilities.

Boeing Computer Services also provides low-cost, high-quality systems, service, and software to targeted manufacturing markets in engineering, scientific,

The Cray Research X-MP conveys a monolithic presence at Boeing Computer Services' data center. The revolutionary supercomputer helps keep Boeing on the cutting edge of scientific and engineering computing technology.

and telecommunications industries. This includes systems integration, networking, facilities management, supercomputing, and professional services.

All Boeing Computer Services facilities and offices are connected by the Boeing Telecommunications Network. Based at Kent, it transmits data by land lines, microwave transmitters, and fiber optics, with an operational availability of more than 99.9 percent. The network also delivers remote computing services to non-Boeing customers in cities worldwide.

Computer equipment at the Bellevue data center includes several computer mainframes and a high-speed, state-of-the-art CRAY supercomputer that can process approximately 90 million calculations per second. The site is also the base for the Information Management Service, designed for on-line interaction applications that have shared files interacting on large-scale mainframe computers.

The Kent data center, located south of Seattle, is at the Boeing Aerospace & Electronics division headquarters. This data center contains 150,000 square feet of office and computing space. The center opened in 1980. The Kent data center houses several large-scale computers to support batch processing and on-line systems.

Primarily serving U.S. government customers, the Vienna, Virginia, data center was opened in 1979. Situated on 34 acres just 15 miles from the nation's capital, it was the first Boeing computer facility designed specifically to house large-scale computers.

The Wichita data center became fully operational in 1986 and supports the operations of Boeing Military Airplanes. The 190,000-square-foot data center is on a 90-acre site adjacent to Boeing's Wichita, Kansas, Military Airplanes plant.

The Huntsville, Alabama, data center became fully opera-

tional in 1986 and supports the operations of Boeing Military Airplanes and Boeing Aerospace & Electronics at Huntsville.

Opened in early 1987, the Philadelphia data center includes 160,000 square feet of data center and office space. The center supports operations at Boeing Helicopters division.

All data centers are protected against service interruption from fire, earthquakes, and other disasters by a combination of engineering features that include backup systems. The physical environment of computer areas is constantly monitored to ensure airflow, temperature, humidity, and other environmental variables remain acceptable. The Bellevue data center can withstand an earthquake measuring 7.5 on the Richter scale, almost four times the area's code requirements.

The Bellevue, Kent, and Vienna data centers are equipped with an uninterruptive power supply backed up by diesel generators. The Wichita, Huntsville, and Philadelphia data centers are equipped with battery-backed uninterruptive power supply units that ensure operation through minor power outages and an orderly shutdown in a major disaster.

Boeing Computer Services

Boeing's Bellevue telecommunications management center monitors and maintains the flow of more than one million voice calls daily, in addition to heavy data, message, and video traffic. Based on digital technology, Boeing's is among the world's largest and most modern private networks.

also is the home of Boeing Advanced Technology Center for Computer Sciences, a focal point for development of artificial intelligence applications. Investigative work by the Advanced Technology Center is dedicated to keeping Boeing at the forefront of the fast-moving computer services industry.

The Advanced Technology Center has undertaken specialized efforts, such as directing Boeing's participation with the Carnegie Group Inc., in which it acquired an equity interest in 1984. The center also sponsors colloquia and oversees the Skill Enhancement Program developed to provide Boeing software engineers with graduate-level training in advanced technology.

Boeing Computer Services' 2,500 Bellevue employees also have invested in the community in which they work, giving their time and donating funds to organizations throughout the Puget Sound.

MICROSOFT CORPORATION

Microsoft is recognized internationally, and the international division represents more than 50 percent of the company's business. Subsidiaries in Germany and France together did nearly twice as much business in 1988 as the company had done in fiscal-year 1983. Future products are being developed with the international market in mind. More than 220 localized versions of Microsoft products are delivered annually to the international market. The firm employs 4,000 worldwide, and approximately 3,000 work at the Redmond headquarters office.

From its giant corporate headquarters at Evergreen Place in Redmond, Microsoft continues to develop software products and computer operating systems that are among the most technically astute. In 1988 Microsoft delivered the first version of the OS/2 operating system—a joint development of Microsoft and IBM. Microsoft OS/2 represents a powerful new platform designed to make the most of the power of the latest microcomputers. This first version laid the

The Microsoft Excel spreadsheet program is one of the company's many industry-standard software products.

William A. Gates and Redmond-based Microsoft Corporation are legends in their own time. The thriving company, which introduced 43 new and enhanced products into the computer software market in 1988, is the brainchild of Gates, who at age 19 started the company with a friend, Paul Allen, who was 21.

It was in 1975 in Albuquerque, New Mexico, that Gates and Allen (who has since left Microsoft and runs his own company) adapted the computer language BASIC for the first personal computer, the Mits-Altair. Microsoft developed a new operating system, called MS-DOS, that was the first computer language for the personal computer. The real significance of that development, however, is that International Business Machines (IBM) selected MS-DOS as the operating system for the IBM-PC in 1981. That decision put Microsoft on the map. By that time Gates had moved the company back to his native Pacific Northwest.

Since then Microsoft's assets have doubled, tripled, quadrupled. The firm reported assets of more

Microsoft employees enjoy a pleasant afternoon break from work at the firm's expansive corporate campus in Redmond.

than $720 million in 1989. In 1988 Microsoft became the first microcomputer software company to earn more than $100 million in revenues in a single quarter. Revenues in fiscal-year 1989 equaled $803.5 million, a 36-percent increase over fiscal 1988 revenues.

groundwork for the development of OS/2 with a graphics-based interface.

Over the years Microsoft has won dozens of awards and received hundreds of excellent reviews for its products. Microsoft Word and Microsoft Excel are among the software products that have made the company famous.

Microsoft develops software for both IBM PC and compatibles and the Apple Macintosh. The firm continues to forge alliances that will establish its strategic position within the industry. The company licenses software to manufacturers in the United States and abroad, including Acer, Compaq, Hewlett-Packard, NCR, NEC, Olivetti, Philips, Tandy, and Zenith.

In addition to software development, Microsoft is also in the publishing business. Microsoft Press, the book-publishing arm of the company, released 30 new titles in 1988. Of the 155-plus titles published in its brief history, 35 have made best-seller lists for computer trade books. Microsoft Press books are printed in 15 languages and sold in more than 50 countries.

How does the company continue to grow this fast and still succeed? The growth of personal computer hardware sales worldwide certainly benefits Microsoft's sales, but much of the firm's success can be attributed to its dedication to research and development. Investment in research and development is essential to maintaining the company's long-term position of leadership within the industry.

Few question that Microsoft has taken and will continue to take the entire industry into a new realm. The company looks ahead to the day when there will be a computer on every desk and in every home. To deliver on this vision, its management has established a series of strategies that focus not only on maximizing short-term gains but also on positioning the corporation for a continuing leadership role in the future of personal computing.

Behind all this work, according to Microsoft's 1988 annual report, must be a commitment to make computers more accessible to more people. By design, Microsoft products bring the best available technology to the broadest base of customers. To do that effectively, the company must give its customers full support to make the most of their products. Microsoft's product support telephone lines received some 750,000 calls in 1988.

"Successful companies need to take intelligent risks and not rest on past successes." This statement, offered in the firm's 1988 annual report, sums up the philosophy that will take the company into the future. Microsoft is aware of what the market demands and is constantly expanding to meet those demands. For example, a manufacturing facility in Dublin, Ireland, has allowed the firm to better meet the needs of the European market.

In a nutshell, Microsoft Corporation's spirit to succeed is representative of the growth on the Eastside itself. The young, rambunctious company compares well with the area in which it operates.

Much of Microsoft's locally produced software is manufactured at the Bothell distribution center on the Eastside.

BORDEN CHEMICAL

Known locally as Borden Chemical, the Adhesives and Resins Division of Borden Inc. has served the forest products and packaging industries from the Puget Sound area since 1932. A small factory in downtown Seattle pioneered the production of synthetic resin adhesives in 1936, adding a new dimension to the woodworking industry.

Acceptance of synthetic resins by the forest products industry was phenomenal, and the company began the manufacture of other chemicals for the industry. In 1946 the division began producing formaldehyde in plants in Springfield, Oregon; Bainbridge, New York; and Demopolis, Alabama.

The Adhesives and Resins Division moved its corporate headquarters to Bellevue in 1970. Today the 45-member staff provides administrative, sales, accounting, accounts payable, purchasing, safety, environmental, and quality-control administration for the division's 20 plants, three laboratories, and 790 employees nationwide. The division produced $304 million in net trade sales in 1988, representing an increase of close to 20 percent over 1987.

Much of the growth of the firm can be traced to its commitment to developing the latest and highest-quality products. Research and development operations are extremely important; one in every 16 employees is engaged in improvement of resin polymer binder systems.

The steady and stable growth of the forest products industry in the Northwest has led Borden to become its largest supplier of resins, adhesives, and binders. The division is nationally known for its quality of production and experience in developing and selling these products.

With the development of synthetic resins back in the 1930s, the plywood industry literally was born in the Puget Sound region.

This led to the opening of the Seattle plant, which was moved to Kent, Washington, in 1961; its efforts are credited with making the region the top competitor in the wood production industry nationwide.

In addition to supplying resins for particle board, hardboard, and softwood plywood, Borden also markets sizing agents, including slack wax and wax emulsions for the particle board, fiberboard, hardboard, and structural panel industries. The company also produces chemical additives, including catalysts, retarders, fillers, and modifiers in both liquid and powder form.

Three of the firm's plants serve the packaging industry with adhesives and binders for such uses as cartons, book binding, and corrugated boards. Robert G. Jenkins, general manager of the division, relates, "The Adhesives and Chemicals Group is committed to being the leader in the development, production, and marketing of resin binder systems and specialty adhesives. Our mission is to provide optimum value to satisfy our customers' needs through innovation, quality products, and customer service."

Borden manufactures a plethora of chemical products in the Northwest because of the area's rich forest resources. Shown here is Borden's National Research and Development lab in Springfield, Oregon, and the adjacent production facility.

In 1988 Borden Adhesives and Resins provided 16.2 percent of its parent company's revenues. Borden Inc., a $7.5-billion organization, has some 47,500 employees worldwide. The diversified firm—first known for its dairy and Elmers Glue-all consumer products—markets pasta, snacks, nonfood consumer goods, and chemical specialties.

The Borden Foundation was established to advance the education of women and minorities. Borden Inc. purchased more than one million dollars in goods and services from minority-owned businesses in 1988.

Locally Borden Adhesives and Resins has been a 100-percent participant of the King County United Way campaign. The company has sponsored scholarships for the forest products industry and has participated in forest product education and research in cooperation with universities in Washington and Oregon.

Photo by Gary Greene

10
BUSINESS AND PROFESSIONS

Greater Bellevue's business and professional community brings a wealth of service, ability, and insight to the area.

Photo by Gary Greene

Bellevue Chamber of Commerce, 144

Dain Bosworth Inc., 145

Seafirst Bank, 146-149

Clark, Nuber and Co., P.S., 150

United Olympic Life Insurance Company, 151

Security Pacific Bank, 152-155

Foster Pepper & Shefelman, 156-157

First Mutual Bank, 158

Revelle, Ries & Hawkins, 159

Key Bank of Puget Sound, 160-161

KPMG Peat Marwick, 162-163

Sweeney Conrad, 164

BELLEVUE CHAMBER OF COMMERCE

An exciting location and uniquely involved volunteers are two characteristics of the Bellevue Chamber of Commerce. Bellevue, Washington, has evolved from the remote, rural community it was in 1953 to a sophisticated center of commerce for the Eastside. Not surprisingly, the Bellevue Chamber of Commerce has grown with the city, and the association's volunteers and staff are at the forefront of regional growth issues such as transportation, kindergarten through grade 12 education, higher education, and governance.

Established in 1929, the Bellevue Chamber of Commerce is today made up of more than 1,600 companies. It is from those firms that the thousands of volunteers who serve on the chamber committees and task forces are drawn.

To carry out its mission of ensuring the business community's economic well-being, the Bellevue Chamber of Commerce has identified several areas of service to its members. The chamber provides issues representation for its members and is a watchdog for each member at all levels of the government. In addition, the organiza-

tion sponsors a wide variety of networking events, such as a monthly luncheon with well-known business leaders as speakers and a Business After Hours that provides a social environment for making business contacts. The chamber's professional development services—brown-bag lunch seminars on timely business topics, half-day seminars with expert speakers, and small business roundtables and counseling—have a reputation of excellence.

More so than in many chambers, policy and programs are developed from the ground up at the Bellevue Chamber of Commerce. Volunteers serving on committees, with the assistance of a specialized staff, prepare recommendations for the board of directors on issues and programs. The 40-member board of directors, the

The Bellevue Chamber of Commerce offices are located on the seventh floor of the Seafirst Building (tall building at right), part of the Bellevue Place complex. Bordered by the Hyatt Regency Bellevue and a seven-story office and retail complex, the chamber is located in the heart of downtown. Courtesy, Whitehill Studio

governing body of the organization, provides the final approval on all proposals. The board annually prepares an action plan that is mandated by the membership.

Themes such as Action is Eloquence and Commitment to Progress have described the chamber's most recent action plans. For the 1989-1990 program year the chairman of the board selected Goals for the Pacific Century. Through its action plans, the chamber tackles vital issues that affect the business community.

Other Bellevue Chamber of Commerce programs and services include a monthly newsletter, free or low-cost marketing publications and research information, advertising and promotion opportunities, and a complete employee benefits package tailored to meet members' needs. The benefits package offers health insurance, life insurance, dental insurance, disability insurance, and a retirement and savings plan.

Members, through their dues, hire the Bellevue Chamber of Commerce staff and volunteer structure to address local, state, and regional issues and to provide valuable programs and services.

DAIN BOSWORTH INC.

Dain Bosworth Inc. believed that Bellevue was destined for dynamic growth in the 1980s. Based on that belief, the firm opened one of its very first Pacific Northwest branch offices in the area in 1983. Today both Bellevue and the company are prospering.

The growth of the Bellevue office has paralleled the growth of Bellevue. In five years the office has more than quadrupled to its current size of 20 investment executives and a support staff of nine.

"We really emphasize client service and are working to be regarded as the Nordstrom of the securities industry," says resident manager Ron Dunlap. "For that reason, we are oriented toward building client relationships, not just product sales."

Dunlap has managed the Dain Bosworth office since its opening. Prior to that he served as King County executive and as Republican leader in the Washington State Legislature.

"The changing financial marketplace presents challenges," says Dain Bosworth president Fred Friswold in Minneapolis. "But superior people coupled with our philosophy of service to our clients are the main reasons the Bellevue office has flourished."

Each Dain Bosworth investment executive brings financial expertise together with top-notch service for the ultimate in client satisfaction.

The Eastside office also serves the Bellevue area in another important way—as a good corporate citizen. Members of the firm's Bellevue staff serve on the boards and committees of such organizations as the United Way, the Boys and Girls Club, the Eastside Rotary Clubs, the Bellevue Art Museum, the Bellevue Chamber of Commerce, and other worthy organizations.

But Dunlap is most proud of the high quality and level of professionalism Dain employees bring to their clients. "We have absolutely top-notch investment executives who really know this business. Each of them offers the complete range of investment vehicles, including tax-free bonds, government bonds, stocks, CDs, and annuity. Further, every one of our service assistants is registered and licensed by the Securities and Exchange Commission (SEC)."

Dain Bosworth's investment executives in Bellevue also work closely with the firm's often-quoted regional research unit located in Seattle. The company's researchers live in the Pacific Northwest and focus on Northwest financial opportunities.

Dain Bosworth Inc. is constantly assessing and reassessing client needs. In that process, active client participation is encouraged. A toll-free hotline allows clients to get quotes and evaluation of their accounts quickly. And the firm's recently revised brokerage statement is clear, concise, and understandable.

Summing it all up, Dunlap says, "We work both with and for our clients. Superior service that goes beyond what might be expected—that's the way we try to do business in Bellevue."

The professional staff at Dain Bosworth brings total service to Bellevue investors.

SEAFIRST BANK

Seafirst Bank, the oldest and largest bank in Washington State, introduced a mission in 1988 that has laid the foundation for many years to come. It is Seafirst's goal to be the premier Northwest bank, providing the highest-quality customer service and achieving superior profitability and dominant market share in the Pacific Northwest personal, business, and real estate markets.

It is a goal the bank has been working toward for some time, and Seafirst's Eastside Division plays an increasingly important role in its success. With 500 Eastside employees and 30 branches, Seafirst's Bellevue operation has established a competitive edge. In fact, Seafirst's entire commercial banking operation is handled from its Eastside Division headquarters office.

Above: Bellevue has changed considerably since the time of this early downtown view. Photo circa 1920s, courtesy, Bellevue Downtown Association

Below: Customers can expect the ultimate in quick service through Seafirst's Excel Service, which features both the Express Teller and a five-minute service guarantee.

States that introduced the elements in one complete package.

Excel features include extended hours (9 a.m. to 6 p.m. each weekday), toll-free 24-hour telephone access to service representatives to handle routine matters such as balance inquiries and funds transfers; additional ATMs in the branches; and an instant five-dollar bill to any customer who has to stand in a teller line more than five minutes. Seafirst was also the first bank in Washington State to introduce Saturday banking, which is now available from 9 a.m. to 1 p.m. Helms emphasizes that this is not a onetime promo-

Seafirst's Bellevue Place branch is indeed the "bank branch of the future," located in the city's premier office-hotel-retail complex.

Seafirst recently opened what *Bank Marketing* called "the bank branch of the future, or at any rate, one version of it." Conceived and operated by Seafirst, the branch is located in Bellevue Place, a new office/hotel/retail complex in downtown Bellevue. The branch occupies approximately 5,000 square feet, has a staff of 10, and opened for business early in 1989. Seafirst president Luke Helms described it then as "probably the most advanced bank branch in the nation right now."

Seafirst's Real Estate Center, which includes residential, commercial, and builder banking, as well as corporate, private, and commercial banking, is located on the third, fourth, and fifth floors of Bellevue Place. In sum, Seafirst occupies more than 57,000 square feet, making it the building's lead tenant. Seafirst is also a limited partner for the project, which was developed by Kemper Freeman of Freeman Development. Seafirst operates its Bellevue Main Branch, which includes a drive-through facility, directly across the street.

Some service features at its

Bellevue-area branches are not unique to the Eastside alone: In early 1989 Seafirst launched a system-wide campaign called Excel to promote enhanced customer service at all its branches statewide. According to Helms, Seafirst was the only bank in the United

tion, rather a "new way of life" at Seafirst as it strives to be the best regional bank in the country.

Seafirst's innovative service standards have helped it achieve what is likely the largest bank market share on the Eastside. Seafirst senior vice-president Larry B.

Stunning architecture and graceful lines adorn Columbia Seafirst Center, headquarters of Seafirst Bank.

lion and $817.6 of shareholder's equity at the end of the second quarter 1989, Seafirst has developed a reputation for excellence in the Puget Sound. Its roots go back to the 1850s, when Dexter Horton placed a coffee barrel in his general store that served as the first depository for loggers, trappers, farmers, and merchants who lived and worked in Seattle.

In 1870 Horton purchased a safe and, with David Phillips, organized the bank of Phillips, Horton and Company. When Phillips died, Arthur Denny purchased his interest, and the name was changed to Dexter Horton and Company. For the next 10 years it was the only bank in Seattle.

In 1929, nine Seattle banks merged, including Dexter Horton National Bank, the First National Bank Group, and Seattle National Bank. They later changed their name to First National Bank of Seattle. Spokane and Eastern Trust Company was merged with the First

Excel service means that Seafirst customers have toll-free 24-hour telephone access to the bank's service representatives.

Ogg manages the Eastside Division. His mandate is to increase market share, and he says he'll do it by offering the best customer service available.

Even though the bank is large, Ogg says it uses the "niche bank" concept to target its services. For example, Seafirst's new Bellevue branch includes a separate merchant service area for its business customers, offering extended banking hours, a private conference room, and customer telephones. As a result, customers avoid lines and receive service from staff especially trained in retail banking.

Seafirst, a wholly owned subsidiary of Bank America Corporation, claims a banking relationship with 60 percent of the households in Washington State. With headquarters in the Columbia Seafirst Center, Seafirst has more than 168 branches statewide, plus two offices in Portland. At the end of second quarter 1989, Seafirst had $11.1 billion in assets and $8.9 billion in deposits.

With a loan portfolio of $9.3 bil-

National Bank of Seattle in 1935, changing the institution's name to Seattle First National Bank and expanding its services statewide. By 1960 the bank served 64 cities of Washington, with 87 offices throughout the state and total resources of more than one billion dollars. BankAmerica Corporation merged with Seafirst in the early 1980s. Today Seafirst continues to operate by its own local board and management team.

Through the years Seafirst has remained committed to the community, which is evident by its involvement with local arts and human services organizations. On the Eastside, Seafirst has funded and continues to support a number of community projects and organizations, including the Bellevue Art Museum, Bellevue Schools Foundation, Overlake Hospital, Youth Eastside Services, the

Seafirst Volunteers take up paint brushes, hammers, and shovels to help rehabilitate the King Way Apartment Complex in Seattle.

Bellevue Philharmonic, Bellevue Boys and Girls Club, and the Eastside Human Services.

The bank's commitment to its employees is evident as well. Seafirst realizes its people are the single most important resource it has to accomplish its mission, so staff input is constantly encouraged. In 1988 each employee was asked what five things they could personally do to help the bank accomplish its goals. This procedure involved everyone in the success of the company, rather than dictating from the top down.

Since Seafirst realizes the value of a skilled and customer-driven work force, it has invested millions in training to help make

its employees successful. Seafirst College, a series of banking and customer service courses set up and run through the University of Washington's Graduate School of Business, is one example. Some 900 Seafirst employees have graduated from the college since its inception in 1987, and hundreds more are expected to graduate by year-end 1989.

Because its employees are responsible for Seafirst's success, Helms says the bank will continue to provide an environment that encourages accomplishment and enables each person to achieve his or her full potential.

It is this type of innovation and commitment that has set Seafirst Bank ahead in the state's first hundred years and will continue to keep it as the state's most successful bank in the years to come.

CLARK, NUBER AND CO., P.S.

The traditional services provided by accountants are not enough in today's complex economy. Business owners need a broader range of business, tax, and financial management services. Clark, Nuber and Co., P.S., offers such services, backed by sound experience combined with fresh ideas and a motivated, professional staff.

Clark, Nuber president Bob Nuber believes the company became the biggest CPA firm in Bellevue by being the best. The organization has a reputation for providing results-oriented planning for businesses based throughout the Northwest.

Clark, Nuber is nearly as old as the city in which it is headquartered, tracing its beginning to the early 1950s. In 1989 there were 65 employees, 50 who are CPAs, in a company that has designed its practice around growing, entrepreneurial clients. Clark, Nuber provides accounting, tax, business, and computer consulting services to clients with annual revenues ranging from one million dollars to $50 million with consulting projects to even larger businesses.

The firm's typical clients are growing, privately held companies whose owners are involved in their management. Clark, Nuber has developed special expertise in the real estate, construction, manu-

In Clark, Nuber's tax library are Doug Cruikshank, senior tax manager, and Kimberly Snider, tax senior.

facturing, food-service, and professional services industries.

Clark, Nuber professionals work closely with their clients, tailoring solutions to particular needs. Client-service teams are assembled to review each client's business and take a long-term interest in helping them achieve their goals.

Clark, Nuber and Co. is at the forefront of microcomputer applications for business use. The firm has helped many of its clients select and install computer accounting systems and has also designed computerized planning models that produce "what if" analyses with various sales, costs, and cash-flow assumptions to aid in new business ventures or in business expansion. The firm has also helped clients recruit and select key managers, design employee benefit plans, and has consulted on the purchase and sale of businesses.

Clark, Nuber accountants are expert at traditional accounting services, including preparing audit and financial statements and reports. In addition to preparing tax returns for corporations, partnerships, trusts, estates, individuals, and nonprofit organizations, the firm provides tax planning in the

Clark, Nuber shareholders express confidence in the firm and in Bellevue. From left to right are Gary Corum, Dennis Weibling, John Fedor, Bob Nuber, Todd Hatch, Ron Rauch, and Tom Sedlock.

areas of individual tax reduction; the purchase, sale, merger, or dissolution of a business; estate planning; and fringe benefits.

"Bellevue no longer is the bedroom community it used to be," says Nuber, a respected community leader. "It used to be that those who desired more sophisticated work thought they had to go to Seattle. That's no longer the case."

Nuber has worked diligently over the years, serving on boards and committees and presiding over the Bellevue Rotary Club to help the community remain a good place to live and work. He participated in a special United Way effort in 1988-1989 to heighten awareness among Eastside citizens of a range of issues such as poverty and education.

"We're a full-fledged city with many of the problems large cities have to deal with," says Nuber. "We're still ahead of the game; I hope we can keep it that way."

UNITED OLYMPIC LIFE INSURANCE COMPANY

United Olympic Life Insurance Company dates back to 1934, when Olympic National Life Insurance Company was formed to provide insurance to loggers of the old Northwest. From a small waterfront office in Seattle, agents trekked through the region's logging camps selling insurance. Back in those days, life insurance was predominantly a regional concept.

Through the years the clientele expanded, and in 1972 the firm was purchased by Unigard, a Seattle-based property and casualty company. The organization was renamed Unigard Olympic Life Insurance Company and began selling through independent property and casualty agents as well as through its long-standing agent field force.

United Olympic Life Insurance Company, renamed and relocated to Bellevue when sold by Unigard in 1984, is now a wholly owned subsidiary of USLICO, an Arlington, Virginia, life holding company. USLICO was originally founded 50 years ago to provide insurance to military officers and

Developing and marketing life insurance, group insurance, and tax-deferred annuities is the major thrust of United Olympic Life's business development effort.

now is a diversified holding company with subsidiaries involved in insurance, real estate, and banking. The corporation's assets exceed $2 billion.

USLICO's life insurance division comprises four companies that operate in designated geographic regions nationwide. United Olympic Life, the largest company in USLICO's life insurance division, serves what are known as the Pac-10 states. The company reported $650 million in assets by year-end 1988.

Since it was acquired by USLICO, the scope of the Bellevue-based company has changed. While it still sells traditional life insurance, 90 percent of its assets come from annuities. The annuities market has been pegged as a high-growth area by the firm's president James J. Hagerty, who says that an aggressive marketing effort is under way to build on that

strength. At the same time the company has received strong endorsements from agents and customers alike for its affordable individual and group life product lines.

Today United Olympic Life Insurance Company employs 90 people and maintains about 400 general agents and 2,000 soliciting agents throughout its geographic territory.

The A.M. Best Company reviews the financial status of thousands of insurers and gave United Olympic Life Insurance an "A+." This rating reflects Best's opinion of the relative financial strength and operating performance of an insurance company in comparison to the norms of the life/health insurance industry. The company reported $5 billion total insurance in force as of January 1, 1989.

United Olympic Life Insurance Company has carved a well-defined market for itself in Bellevue, and it is comfortable with its headquarters location. Employees are active in community activities, including the United Way, local chambers, and youth sports. The firm was a major contributor to the Bellevue Downtown Park.

The people of United Olympic Life Insurance Company have provided life insurance protection and security more than 55 years.

SECURITY PACIFIC BANK

The Security Pacific Plaza Building in downtown Bellevue, opened in 1986, serves as the bank's Eastside headquarters. Its bold architecture and mirrored facade add dimension to the city's skyline.

fold of banks in California, Arizona, Oregon, Alaska, Nevada, and Washington. With assets exceeding $85 million, Security Pacific Corporation is the fifth-largest banking company in the nation. Rainier Bank was renamed Security Pacific Bank Washington on January 1, 1989.

Name changes have been an integral part of the bank's history. More than 100 years ago founder Robert R. Spencer intended to call the firm Seattle Banking Company, but, because he wanted to attract Tacoma customers, he decided to name it Bank of Commerce. In 1890 Spencer secured a national bank charter and renamed the institution National Bank of Commerce of Seattle.

In 1906 the bank merged with Washington National Bank. The bank's name was not changed, which always was a bone of contention for the new management.

In 1928 National Bank of Commerce merged with Marine Bancorporation, a bank holding company led by its founder Andrew Price. National Bank of Commerce and Marine retained their own names for more than 40 years until events forced a reevaluation of the names of both the holding company and bank.

Marine Bancorporation stock had been reorganized, and the company felt the need to make its name better known. Confusion caused some potential investors to look for the stock under National Bank of Commerce, rather than Marine. Others confused Marine Bancorporation with other banking organizations using Marine in their name. In 1972 the institution's advertising agency and some senior officers proposed changing the name of the holding

The history of Security Pacific Bank Washington is colorful and interesting, complex and intriguing. In fact, the bank's first 80 years is the subject of a comprehensive book that was published in 1976. As the bank completes its 100th year of service, a second, updated history book, called *Banking Without Boundaries*, is now on bookstore shelves.

Established in Seattle as the National Bank of Commerce in 1889, three months before Washington became the 42nd state in the union, the institution has evolved from territorial banking to worldwide banking. For 83 years it was known as the National Bank of Commerce of Seattle and was renamed Rainier Bank in 1973.

In 1987 Los Angeles-based Security Pacific Corporation acquired Rainier Bank, merging it into its company to NB of C Bancorporation. They thought the acronym already had a good identity locally, and its official widespread use would end the confusion.

But not everyone liked the idea. Director Prentice Bloedel expressed misgivings over the use of an acronym. The decision of what to call the bank was put off another year when G. Robert Truex, Jr., was named president and chief executive officer of Marine in September 1973. He announced at the annual meeting in 1974 that the company had hired a corporate identity consultant to help it find a new name.

"It takes a steel spine to change your name," Truex told stockholders. Truex personally leaned toward the name "Rainier," which had been suggested to him by a friend. After a few months Rainier was the name recommended for the bank and the holding company.

Whether cashing a check or buying stocks and bonds, customers can find all the financial services they are looking for at the Security Pacific Plaza branch in downtown Bellevue. The same services are available at any of the 15 Security Pacific branches on the Eastside.

Selling the name to the board and to customers wasn't as easy. After the name was officially adopted in November 1974, angry mail began pouring in. The event marked the rare occasion when a bank underwent a name change without a merger or acquisition.

About 14 years later, in October 1988, Rainier Bank directors voted to change the name of the

Heading up Security Pacific's team on the Eastside are (from left to right): James M. Sheeley, vice-president and regional manager for private banking; Jean F. Miller, vice-president and manager for corporate banking; and Joseph P. Zavaglia, senior vice-president and manager of the Eastside Region.

bank to Security Pacific Bank Washington and the holding company to Security Pacific Bancorporation Northwest. "Despite the equity in the Rainier name, the new name reflects the modern era of deregulated interstate banking," says chairman and chief executive officer John D. Mangels.

At first, customers of Rainier Bank hardly noticed the bank's change in ownership—but it didn't take them long to realize the benefits of banking with such a large and diverse company with sophisticated banking services and products.

When the bank officially changed its name in January 1989, customers had already grown to trust the organization that employs some 42,000 people in 46 states and 27 countries. With more than 1,500 locations and 1,000 automated teller machines nationwide,

Security Pacific Corporation offers Washington customers a level of service they never dreamed existed. Rainier's customers accepted the name change with barely a ripple of protest.

Truex was a great influence on Rainier Bank and helped it establish a state presence. The Eastside became a substantial market for the bank in the early 1980s. Today Security Pacific employs more than 400 people on the Eastside, where its retail and consumer business has increased as much as 30 percent since 1986.

More than 250 of the bank's Eastside employees work at the sleek Security Pacific Plaza (formerly Rainier Plaza), in downtown Bellevue. Completed in 1986, the building houses several Security Pacific units, including private banking, corporate banking, retail banking, financial management, trust services, and the Dealer Fi-

The 40-story Security Pacific Tower, with its unique pedestal design, has been a Seattle landmark since 1977. The tower is the main office for Security Pacific's operations in Washington, Oregon, and Alaska.

nance Center. Now the headquarters office of the Eastside, it provides customers with services they might have otherwise had to go to downtown Seattle to get.

In 1988 the bank launched a pilot in-store banking program. Today more than a dozen Safeway Stores in western Washington have full-service Security Pacific branches. Safeway branches offer consumers the convenience of banking while shopping for groceries.

Security Pacific Bank Washington offers customers automated teller machines (ATMs) worldwide. The bank was one of the original founders of the EXCEL system in the early 1970s. Today Security Pacific customers can use more than 17,220 ATMs in 47 states, Canada, Japan, and the United Kingdom.

Security Pacific Bank Washington has an aggressive plan to expand its market share with better services and new products. The bank is a leading provider of private banking for customers with complex financial needs. The service, offered on the Eastside since 1982 to address the financial needs of the upscale consumer market, includes total banking services, customized credit products, investment products, portfolio management services, and personal financial management.

The Investment Center in downtown Seattle was opened in 1988 to bring Wall Street closer to customers. Investors can stop by the center to glance at the latest market quotes from the New York Stock Exchange or find out how local stocks are faring. But the center isn't just for those who buy stocks. Sophisticated investors, as well as first-time buyers, can purchase CDs, government securities, municipal bonds, gold and silver, and a host of other products. Customers can set up trust accounts, meet with a financial planner, or talk with their personal banker at the Investment Center.

Financial Management and

Security Pacific's Investment Center in downtown Seattle attracts investors seeking the latest news from Wall Street. Using Quotron terminals, investors can obtain quotes on individual stocks and mutual funds, and place a buy or sell order right on the spot. The Dow Jones readerboard (background) gives up-to-the-minute news on the direction of the overall market.

Trust Services, located on the Eastside, provides investment services—including annuities and mutual funds—for private and business clients and personal trust services and tax services for individuals.

The Dealer Finance Center in Bellevue, one of the state's largest, handles the leasing and floor planning for local automobile dealerships. The bank also helps dealerships establish loan programs for car buyers.

The retail banking segment of Security Pacific is among the

man, is an Eastside resident. Two years ago a survey of Eastside consumers rated the bank number one in service. Getzelman and the bank's Eastside management are striving to keep that rating.

Security Pacific may be a new name to the region, but the bank's tradition of community involvement started by NB of C, and carried on by Rainier, continues. Across the Northwest, Security Pacific employees are delivering meals to shut-ins, assisting high school students with homework, and combating child abuse. Many of these projects are accomplished through SecuriTeam Washington, established in 1989, whose more than 900 employee-members have donated several thousand hours to community activities.

Security Pacific Bank Washington continues its leadership role by providing affordable housing in the Seattle area. Through its Community Service Corporation and Home Loan Center, the bank has financed the construction or rehabilitation of several apartment units, including the Annapolis Apartments near downtown Seattle.

Security Pacific Bank actively supports several Eastside organizations and charities, including Ronald McDonald House, Bellevue Downtown Association, Bellevue Community College Foundation, the Bellevue Art Museum, and Bellevue Chamber of Commerce. In fact, the bank is so committed to community service that it has become a part of its employee review criteria. Senior employees are queried annually about their community service efforts and are encouraged to become and stay involved in the community they serve.

Security Pacific Bank Washington enters the 1990s under the management team of chairman John D. Mangels and president John C. Getzelman.

company's strongest units, meeting its customers' needs with high-quality personal service. Branches cater to individual and business clients, and the bank has opened several small-business banking centers to better serve those clients. These centers will be operated from select branches statewide and will be geared to handle the needs of these closely held companies.

Through the corporate banking unit of Security Pacific Washington larger companies can access almost any type of commercial product available in the world of banking today. Much of the focus of this unit is on the Eastside, where the institution's management has targeted new growth.

Indicative of the commitment to the Eastside is the fact that the bank's president, John C. Getzel-

FOSTER PEPPER & SHEFELMAN

The Bellevue office of Foster Pepper & Shefelman provides Eastside individuals, businesses, and municipalities with the personal service of a small law firm and the experience and full range of services of a large, nationally recognized law firm. Foster Pepper & Shefelman's clients are as varied in size and character as the legal services they require. The firm represents some of the Pacific Northwest's fastest growing companies and also serves many smaller businesses, governments, and individuals. At Foster Pepper & Shefelman, every client is important.

The Bellevue office, which now comprises 16 attorneys, 3 paralegals, and 14 support staff, was opened in 1982. The office was strengthened in 1986 as the result of a merger with Drake & Whiteley, an eight-lawyer Eastside law firm. In addition, the Bellevue office draws upon the assets of a large and diverse pool of legal talent from the remainder of the

firm, which includes 128 attorneys in four cities and three states.

Although the roots of the firm go deep into Seattle's history, Foster Pepper & Shefelman was formed in 1988, when two of Seattle's oldest law firms merged. The merger of Foster, Pepper & Riviera, established in 1921, and Roberts and Shefelman, established in 1904, provided increased opportunities for the combined firm to more fully satisfy the diverse and changing needs of its Pacific Northwest clients.

Foster Pepper & Shefelman has developed areas of practice that include banking, business law and planning, corporate finance, creditors' rights, estate and personal planning, health and hospital law, international law, labor-management relations, land use

---

At the Bellevue office conference room are, from left, partners Ted Coulson, Diane Istvan, Bill Erxleben, David Wilson, and Kent Whiteley.

and environmental law, litigation and alternative dispute resolution, municipal and local governmental law, public finance, real estate law, securities law, and taxation.

The experience of the Eastside office is concentrated in the areas of business law, taxation and estate planning for individuals and small businesses, real estate and land use law, corporate and securities transactions, high-technology licensing, health care law, and international law.

One-third of Foster Pepper & Shefelman's Eastside attorneys have substantial experience in business planning, taxation, and estate planning. Two attorneys are certified financial planners, and four are CPAs. From simple wills to sophisticated executive compensation packages, tax and estate planning have become key elements of the Eastside office.

In general, the firm is strongest and best known for its work in real estate and land use. In

some form, the firm has represented almost every major developer in the Northwest. The Bellevue office handles many local firms on this front, and one attorney is totally dedicated to keeping current on land use issues and strategy. As the preeminent real estate law firm in the region, Foster Pepper & Shefelman has developed solid relationships with key related agencies and can offer expertise in commercial development, syndication, multifamily residential development, and low-income housing. The firm prides itself on its ability to offer quality service in a cost-effective manner and handles many real estate projects for a fixed fee.

The Bellevue office dedicates a strong portion of its practice to corporate securities transactions, including mergers and acquisitions, financing, and stock options. From representation of start-up firms to large publicly held companies, Foster Pepper & Shefelman's Eastside office is well positioned to assist in business transactions of virtually any size or degree of complexity.

The Eastside office has developed a reputation for its skill in technology licensing and representation of high-technology companies. The office has developed a particular skill in software licensing work, which the firm views as a high-growth area for the Eastside operation.

The Eastside office provides legal services for several prominent regional medical groups, as well as for individual physicians. The firm has been successful in developing innovative methods for medical groups and doctors to structure their practices. The office also represents a variety of large health care businesses.

With the growth of the Eastside and the incidence of international business transactions, the Bellevue office is becoming prominent in international business, han-

dling transactions for firms with interests in China and Taiwan. The firm views the area as one that will continue to grow.

The Eastside office has developed a litigation practice, with two partners specializing in this area. The office also emphasizes its services to small businesses and individual clients. Because the core of its business came from the small firm, small clients are not intimidated by the office's regional presence. The Eastside office is not merely an appendage of the Seattle office, yet when it needs to call on the breadth of experience of that office, it can.

The staff of the Bellevue of-

Foster Pepper & Shefelman's Bellevue office attorneys, paralegals, and staff members pose for a photo outside the Security Pacific Plaza Building.

fice of Foster Pepper & Shefelman is young, creative, and full of energy. Recent installation of a state-of-the-art computer system helps the group stay efficient and lean. The firm's attorneys speak to numerous local, regional, and national groups, and many teach and offer assistance to a variety of continuing-education programs. The firm encourages individual professional development and appreciates its employees' dedication to the community.

FIRST MUTUAL BANK

First Mutual Bank was chartered in 1953, the year Bellevue was incorporated as a city. The first board of the city's first savings and loan comprised a group of people who now are considered the region's founding fathers, including Elwell Case, JYC Kellogg, Herb Mekte, and Kemper Freeman, Sr.

By the end of its first year of operation, the savings and loan reported assets of just under $2 million. Because there was no thrift or bank branch on the Eastside, the small operation began making some loans to people who bought land and built homes in Bellevue. The savings and loan developed quite a following and began financing much of the residential development that earned the area its designation as a bedroom community of Seattle.

In 1967 the state legislature enhanced the mutual savings bank charter, and in 1968 the institution received a savings bank charter. The name was changed to First Mutual Savings Bank, and it was the second savings bank in the state to offer checking accounts. Aggressively pursuing consumer business, the bank became an innovator in customer service. It was one of the first in the nation to offer automated teller service and also one of the founders of The Exchange System.

By the early 1980s First Mutual Bank was entrenched in the community. As the skyline of Bellevue grew, so did the bank, and it had become one of the leading mortgage lenders in the state. Unfortunately, double-digit interest rates on loans and lower savings rates were almost too much for the institution. The years 1981 and 1982 were difficult ones for First Mutual, and by year-end 1982 there was a potential for it to be merged with another institution.

Kemper Freeman, Jr., took two plans to the banking supervisor: One was a merger agreement and the other was a business plan to take the bank into mortgage banking. The supervisor gave the bank the opportunity to turn itself around. In 1982 First Mutual modified its lending program to include mortgage banking and began accepting a higher volume of loans.

Bruce Baker was hired as president of First Mutual, and since early 1983 the bank has been getting stronger. A new management team was brought in to help market services and identify specific areas that needed to be served. In 1985 the institution converted from a mutual savings bank to a stock savings bank. In 1988 it paid stockholders a 20-percent dividend.

That same year a specialized group of potential customers was identified, and First Mutual began a loan program to investors in small apartment and commercial properties. With the advantage of hindsight, the bank identified this area as one of growth, and in three years has developed a $50-million loan portfolio that averages about $350,000 per customer.

Today the bank reports assets of close to $186 million and a customer loyalty that is unequalled. Though it no longer is the largest bank in the community, Baker says First Mutual strives to be the best. "There's danger in trying to be the biggest, but great satisfaction with working toward being the best," he adds.

One of the city's active volunteers, Baker has presided over the Bellevue Art Museum Board, the Boy Scouts of America Council, Japan Week, and the Bellevue Chamber of Commerce in 1989. He says community service is second nature to First Mutual Bank, its founders, and its employees. "In a community such as this, where there is so much going on, people have to take time to keep things moving forward."

Serving the Eastside since 1953, First Mutual Bank boasts assets of close to $186 million and unparalleled customer service.

REVELLE, RIES & HAWKINS

Revelle, Ries & Hawkins, P.S., is the Eastside's largest law firm, providing a full range of professional legal services to its diverse clientele. The firm was created by a combination of lawyers from two long-standing local firms. Its attorneys have been advocates and advisers for Eastside businesses and residents for more than a decade.

Today Revelle, Ries & Hawkins provides its clients with legal assistance ranging from the resolution of complex corporate legal problems to estate planning and family matters, such as dissolution, custody, and adoption. The firm has grown as the Eastside has grown, expanding its legal services to meet the needs of the changing community. Today it represents many of the area's largest and most respected businesses and remains proud of its continued prominence in the fields of business, real estate, technology, and construction law.

The lawyers of Revelle, Ries & Hawkins provide service to institutional lenders, mortgage companies, title insurance companies, developers, commercial and residential real estate companies, as well as the Washington Association of Realtors and the Seattle-King County Board of Realtors. Its subsidiary, Revelle, Ries & Hawkins Escrow, Inc., maintains the state's largest non-institutional escrow operation, handling thousands of commercial and residential real estate transactions every year.

The firm works with businesses in manufacturing, high-tech, retail, and service industries, as well as in areas of hazardous waste and environmental law. Its services include the drafting and negotiation of contracts and business formation, acquisition, merger, financing, liquidation, and dissolution.

The firm's attorneys are experienced in different methods of dispute resolution. They practice in all local, state, and federal courts and governmental agencies, and they also handle cases in arbitration.

The attorneys and staff at Revelle, Ries & Hawkins share a common goal to serve both their clients and the interests of the actively changing Eastside community. Many of the firm's professionals spend their personal time participating in a variety of community activities and volunteering for local organizations.

Many of Bellevue's largest and most prominent firms trust the legal counsel provided by the attorneys of Revelle, Ries & Hawkins.

KEY BANK OF PUGET SOUND

Key Bank of Puget Sound is the result of a merger of Seattle Trust & Savings Bank and First NorthWest Bancorporation. New York-based KeyCorp purchased the two Seattle institutions in 1987, forming Key Bank of Puget Sound, with assets of about one billion dollars and 31 branches throughout the region, one-third of which are on the Eastside.

Plans for the Key Bank of Puget Sound include further expansion on the Eastside, as well as an increase in assets. William H. Stevens, chairman, has charted a course that involves increasing the assets of the bank to $2.5 billion over the next three years.

The North Creek office in the Bothell/Woodinville high-tech corridor is the first new branch established by Key Bank of Puget Sound and a part of the planned effort for further Eastside expansion. The office provides commercial and consumer lending services and deposit products to individuals and small to medium-size businesses in the corridor's three south-end business parks and surrounding communities of Bothell, Woodinville, and Mill Creek. The first full-service commercial bank to open in the corridor, the branch is in an area that houses more than 120 businesses employing in excess of 4,000 people.

"Recognizing the potential that exists on the Eastside, we have focused much of our efforts here in developing business both in consumer and commercial markets," says Stevens. Over the past three years Key Bank has transferred its Mortgage Division from downtown Seattle to Bellevue. The bank has also established an Eastside Commercial Banking Center to manage the rapidly expanding commercial-lending requirements in east King County, according to Stevens.

Key Bank senior vice-president Richard C. Sproul manages the growing east region, which he says is "where the action is.

"The facts are, if you're going to be a significant player, you need to be where the action is. And the action is here on the Eastside," Sproul says. Currently Key Bank of Puget Sound employs 650 people throughout the region, 150 of whom work on the Eastside.

Although Key Bank of Puget Sound is a relatively new bank to the region, its heritage dates back to the turn of the century. Originally chartered as Seattle Trust & Title Company in 1905, Seattle Trust was established to administer trusts and estates during the flurry of the Alaska gold rush. In 1920 it was merged with the Title Trust Company of Seattle, then combined with the investment banking firm of Baillargeon, Winslow & Company in 1930.

After the Bank Holiday of 1933, the culmination of heavy runs on banks, Seattle Trust became the first bank of deposit that was licensed to reopen. Four years later Tower Savings Bank was acquired and became the first branch office of the bank. Several more branches were added during the 1950s, starting the trend of rapid growth that continued into the next decade in the suburbs of Seattle and farther south.

In 1968 Seattle Trust was the first bank in the Northwest to introduce the MasterCard credit card program. At the time the bank was acquired by KeyCorp, Seattle Trust was a full-service commercial bank with 25 branches.

First NorthWest Bancorporation was established in 1972 as the Ballard Bank of Washington. Chartered in 1981, the institution was established to capitalize on the expanding fishing industry in the Norwegian community of Ballard.

Hans Harjo, who had worked for Seattle Trust for 12 years and was president of First NorthWest, is now president and chief executive officer of Key Bank of Puget Sound. Because he knows the people of both banks and the markets they serve, his leadership has been instrumental in the new ownership of the bank.

Stevens brings leadership skills to the region from his previous position as president of Key Bank of Central New York. In his tenure there, Stevens almost doubled the bank's assets, number of employees, and number of branches. "I am very proud of this organization and proud of the overall attitude and skills of our people," Stevens says. "Over the past [year] the bank has shown great resiliency to adapt. We have taken difficulties and turned them into opportunities, and now we are moving forward."

Key Bank of Puget Sound operates from Key Tower in the heart of Seattle's financial district. The bank is a subsidiary of KeyCorp, a $1.5-billion financial services company headquartered in Albany, New York. The firm has focused its banking expansion activities in the Northeast and the Northwest. Following a middle-market focus, KeyCorp has concentrated its resources in cities and smaller communities of the northern tier of states, avoiding overcrowded marketplaces and single-industry loan exposure.

As Bellevue grows into the 1990s, Key Bank of Puget Sounds grows with it, emerging as an Eastside leader in consumer and commercial banking.

KPMG PEAT MARWICK

Security Pacific Plaza is home to KPMG Peat Marwick on the Eastside.

telecommunications, operations and manufacturing management, information technology, marketing/communications, and strategic planning. Central to the delivery of quality service is the service team concept. In this program, the audit, tax, and consulting client service team develops a comprehensive plan that documents the client's key challenges and then introduces the resources necessary to meet those needs. From start-up through maturity, Peat Marwick offers Eastside companies a complete package of services.

The office is perhaps best known for the services it provides to its clients in the high-technology industry that was pioneered by the founding Bellevue professionals. A key to success has been to deliver superior service through a thorough understanding of the high-technology industry. Knowing the industry translates into knowing the client's competition, strengths, and challenges. It means anticipating trends, staying ahead of legislative and regulatory issues as they affect the client's operations, and offering ideas and services that can help a client grow and manage his or her business more profitably.

Exclusive alliances have been established with two premier firms serving the high-technology industry: Regis McKenna, Inc. (RMI), and Pittiglio Rabin Todd & McGrath (PRTM). RMI is the preeminent firm assisting technology-based companies with strategic marketing and communications programs. It opened its Bellevue office in Peat Marwick's space in 1987. Immediately becoming a part of the Eastside infrastructure, it works with industry organizations such as the Washington Software Associa-

KPMG Peat Marwick's office in Security Pacific Plaza radiates high energy. The pace is quick, and the atmosphere projects excitement. The members of the management team, assembled in the comfortable conference room with its sweeping view of the Olympic Mountain Range, can best be described as innovators.

The decision to open a Bellevue office was made in 1982 to provide Eastside clients easy access to the firm's world-class resources. The partner and two managers originally responsible for building the business established the tradition

of an entrepreneurial spirit. This spirit continues in the professionals selected to serve in the Bellevue office today. These professionals thrive in the rapidly changing environment of the growing Eastside companies they serve. Their commitment to serving clients of all sizes has taken this office from its three-room beginnings to occupying an entire floor of the plaza with an option on additional space.

Peat Marwick provides traditional audit and tax accounting services as well as business consulting expertise in financial management,

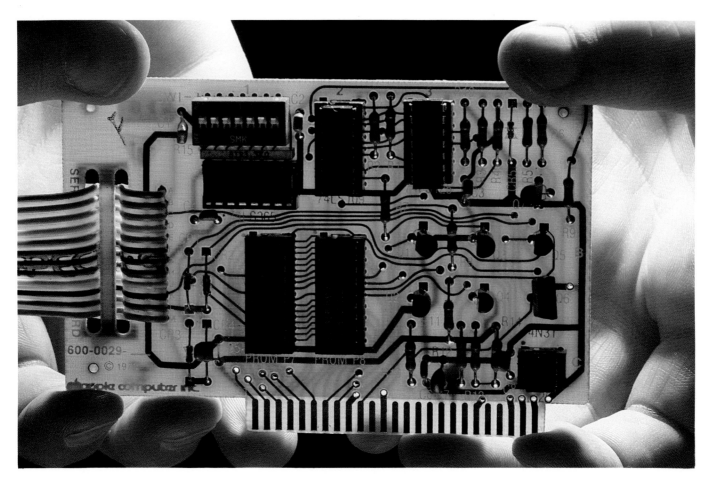

tion to support the economic development of the area. PRTM is a leading provider of manufacturing operations consulting services to technology-based companies. Working through Peat Marwick's office, it provides technology-based companies with the resources to meet manufacturing challenges of the future. The combined range of services offers Bellevue companies an unparalleled wealth of industry knowledge.

The local high-technology practice has become part of the industry infrastructure. Its professionals have been founding members of organizations such as the Washington Software Association, the Northwest Biotechnology Series, and the MIT Enterprise Forum. Monthly breakfast meetings are held for clients and friends of the firm to address topics pertinent to the industry. Meeting topics have included Doing Business in Japan, Strategic Cost Management, and Just-In-Time Manufacturing.

Building from the success of the high-technology practice, spe-cialized industry expertise evolved in the areas of manufacturing, health care, real estate and construction, hospitality, financial institutions, and government services. Experience in these industries makes Peat Marwick uniquely qualified to understand the particular needs of expanding Bellevue companies and serve them in preparing for the challenges of the future.

With such strong local resources Peat Marwick can offer its clients responsive, professional services. Add to this its unequalled geographic coverage as the largest international accounting and consulting firm, and Bellevue has the highest-quality professional services available.

The global marketplace offers Bellevue companies opportunities for growth and profit. However, developing the resources to gain a global perspective is an expensive investment. Through its network of 650 offices in 115 countries, Peat Marwick can respond to Bellevue clients' needs anywhere in the world. Bellevue plays an active

Bellevue's burgeoning high-tech industry is served by the firm's professionals, many of whom are experts in a wide range of technical disciplines.

role in its international network of offices because of its proximity to Canada and the Pacific Rim. As a result there is a commitment to bringing a global perspective to its local clients.

The firm's professionals have firsthand experience in understanding what it means to serve clients in the global marketplace. Many of them work with clients who have international operations. Services to these clients have included assisting with the due diligence for acquisitions of foreign operations, analyzing the impact of local taxes on international operations, and assisting with the successful negotiation of a complex product development agreement with a Japanese company. KPMG Peat Marwick offers an unrivaled combination of local market strength with a cohesive and balanced global network.

SWEENEY CONRAD

In 1980 five ambitious certified public accountants combined their talents to form their own firm in Bellevue. All five had previously worked for more than a decade for a national accounting firm.

"We saw a need to provide principal-to-principal, owner-to-owner accounting services to privately owned companies in the Northwest," says Dennis Conrad. "We believed that these companies in particular weren't efficiently served by the Big Eight firms, and there was an opportunity for another local firm to provide sophisticated services to this business sector."

On that premise, Dennis Conrad, Mike Sweeney, Doug Klan, Kermit Anderson, Ken Johnson, and eventually a sixth partner, Fred Shanafelt, sharpened their pencils and began providing personalized and knowledgeable tax, audit, accounting, and consulting services to business and individuals. Today Sweeney Conrad is one of the largest locally owned certified public

Providing personalized tax, audit, accounting, and consulting services to Bellevue's privately owned businesses are the partners of Sweeney Conrad (from left): Doug Klan, Dennis Conrad, Kermit Anderson, Ken Johnson, Fred Shanafelt, and Mike Sweeney.

accounting firms in the region.

The firm attributes its rapid growth to its overall focus: to provide quality tax, auditing, and consulting services to privately held businesses on a timely basis. Partners with more than 17 years' experience actively lead a team of accountants on each client engagement. This team approach has helped the firm establish credibility quickly. A commitment to offer the finest service available has been instrumental in the development of an outstanding reputation.

Sweeney Conrad's clients encompass all sectors of private industry and include companies with sales ranging from less than one million dollars to $150 million annually. The firm offers the best in accounting services to these clients, including assistance with long-range planning, income tax needs of both the company and its owners or executives, merger and acquisition assistance, and general business consulting.

Indicative of the firm's commitment to Bellevue, Sweeney Conrad developed and built its headquarters office on a woodsy site on 112th Avenue. Now an owner instead of a tenant, the firm discovered that an accessible

location and ample parking are attractive to clients, who can avoid the traffic and parking hassles of a downtown location.

One might assume that, as busy as they have been building their practice, the partners would have little time for community service. In fact, the company is extremely proud of the hundreds of nonbillable hours its employees give the community and the profession. Partners and staff serve on a variety of local boards and committees, including the University of Washington Accounting Development Fund and Accounting Advisory Panel, the Bellevue Downtown Association, the Bellevue Transportation Management Association, the Bellevue Art Museum, local chambers of commerce, and the Chief Seattle Council Boy Scouts of America. One partner is currently serving as president of the Washington Society of Certified Public Accountants, the state's 6,500-member professional association. "It may sound trite, but we believe that if we benefit from the community, we need to give something back," says Conrad. "As long as we have the time and our expertise is needed, we will give."

Photo by Gary Greene

11

BUILDING THE EASTSIDE

From concept to completion, Bellevue's building industry shapes tomorrow's skyline.

Photo by Wolfgang Kaehler

Quadrant Corporation, 168-169

HNTB, 170-171

CH2M HILL, 172-173

SDL Corporation, 174-175

Lease Crutcher Lewis, 176-177

Mithun Partners, 178-179

Wilsey & Ham Pacific, Inc., 180

QUADRANT CORPORATION

From his well-appointed office over-looking the Cascade Mountain Range, Jim Fitzgerald admits that he loves the Pacific Northwest. A Bellevue native, Fitzgerald has witnessed the phenomenal, yet planned, growth of the town in which he grew up and now has a hand in deciding the development of. As president and chief executive officer of the Quadrant Corporation, Fitzgerald manages one of the largest real estate development companies in the Northwest.

Quadrant, a wholly owned subsidiary of Weyerhaeuser Real Estate Company, is a developer and builder of master-planned business parks and residential communities in Washington, Oregon, and California. In the Puget Sound region, Quadrant has developed real estate valued in excess of $173 million.

The history of the city of Bellevue parallels the history of the Quadrant Corporation. For more than three decades the company and the city have experienced robust growth and prosperity. In the early 1950s, when Bellevue was incorporated, businessmen Dick Willard and George Bell founded five companies: Interlake Realty, Western Construction, Interlake Properties, Dick Willard and Associates, and Sherwood Development. A sixth company, Mackey, Moot & Steward, was later acquired. These businesses were primarily engaged in the development and sale of residential real estate. In 1969 the six were merged to form Quadrant Corporation, a move that was described in the *Seattle Post-Intelligencer* this way: "Quadrant will

The sleek Quadrant Plaza, at N.E. Eighth Street and 112th Avenue, is the headquarters for Bellevue's premier integrated real estate developer.

thus bridge all steps in land acquisition, development, planning and zoning, building, financing, engineering, marketing, and merchandising, all under one roof."

That same year Quadrant's 100 employees moved into the new Quadrant Building at N.E. Eighth Street and 112th Avenue, which the newspaper reported was "the newest and brightest landmark in what can become Bellevue's new Realty Row."

Late in 1969 Weyerhaeuser Company announced its acquisition of Quadrant. During the next 10 years Quadrant became one of the area's premier home builders, constructing several thousand new homes.

In 1974 Quadrant added a commercial development division and began the development of West Campus, one of the region's most ambitious projects. The master-planned community in

south King County is a vibrant residential, retail, and business/financial center. This 1,600-acre community comprises more than 500 single-family residences, 1,400 apartments, 650 condominiums, and more than 50 buildings that house approximately 200 businesses. When completed, it is estimated that 18,000 people will live and work there.

Today the commercial development division of Quadrant is a major contributor to the firm's success. The division has 20 major office, light industrial, and retail projects under development in the Seattle, Portland, San Francisco, and Sacramento areas. Locally, Quadrant is developing the Quadrant Business Park in Bothell, the Quadrant Lake Union Center in Seattle, the Auburn Park of Industry, Auburn 400 Corporate Park, the Quadrant Tech Center in Redmond, and the Willows Business Center/Quad 95 in Redmond. The company completed its headquarters office, Quadrant Plaza, a nine-story mid-rise building in downtown Bellevue in the spring

Hunter's Ridge in Issaquah offers home owners large, aesthetically pleasing homes with rich landscapes.

---

of 1988. The new facility was built on the same site as the original Quadrant headquarters, constructed in 1969.

Quadrant maintains offices in Portland and Sacramento. In Portland, Quadrant has developed close to 700,000 square feet of space with an assessed land, office, and industrial space value of $76 million. In California, Quadrant is developing 753,480 square feet of retail, office, and industrial space that will be valued at more than $56 million when completed.

Although there is a heavy emphasis on commercial development, Quadrant is still one of the largest residential land developers in the region. The firm is currently developing 15 residential projects, including West Campus in Federal Way, Remington in Kent, Heritage Hills in Redmond, Hampton Woods in Redmond, Hunter's Ridge in Issaquah, and Northridge

in the Bear Creek area of Redmond. In 1988 Quadrant received five prestigious MAME awards, the Oscar of the home-building industry, for its excellence in home design and marketing.

Fitzgerald said Quadrant Corporation is continually reviewing development opportunities locally as well as in other targeted regions. The company continues to diversify its development, both in location and in product. Locally, Quadrant owns or controls more than 3,000 acres in the planning stage for future development. Another master-planned community is on the drawing boards, and the firm has added multifamily development to its capability, but Fitzgerald intends to keep growth in perspective.

The issue of growth, both as a company and as a community, is important to Fitzgerald. A board member of six organizations that are all wrestling with growth issues, Fitzgerald hopes to help city and regional leaders find ways to accommodate growth without stifling it.

HNTB

Howard Needles Tammen & Bergendoff, commonly referred to as HNTB, celebrates its 75th anniversary in 1989. HNTB maintains some 40 offices nationwide, and the firm billed more than $160 million in 1988. Founded in 1914 in Kansas City, Missouri, HNTB expanded to the Pacific Northwest in 1961, when it received a contract to work on the Hood Canal Bridge. On completion of that project, the partners decided the region was viable enough to support a local office.

In 1974 HNTB merged with Frankfurter and Associates, a Seattle engineering firm specializing in the pulp and paper industry. HNTB then began providing engineering services to both industrial and transportation clients. In 1980 management decided to move the operation to Bellevue. Today the office employs a staff of some 110 people in one of the company's largest offices.

One of HNTB's local claims to fame is its efforts on the Mount Baker Tunnel, the largest-diameter soft bore tunnel in the world. The design of the tunnel earned HNTB the American Consulting Engineers Council's highest award in 1987.

Further, HNTB has developed a great reputation for its work in the field of aviation. The company is currently working with the Federal Aviation Administration in the development of FAA facilities at a second airport in the Denver area.

Architectural services were added to the firm's offerings in 1979. Among the most noted projects attributed to HNTB architects was the design of the Columbus Pavilion at St. Cabrini Hospital. The hospital wanted to add a surgery facility to perform delicate operations, such as eye surgery. Available land was scarce, so HNTB architects proposed an add-on to the top of an existing parking garage. Another architectural contract is the design of the new Bellevue Convention Center, the city's first such facility.

HNTB's Civil/Transportation Department has a long-established tradition of excellence in roadway planning and engineering. A full range of services is provided, including transportation planning; traffic studies; pavement management system studies; alternatives and feasibility analysis; traffic signal planning and design; preliminary and final design of roadways, rail, and transit facilities; environmental assessments; and traffic management plans.

Above: The graceful steel Alsea Bay Bridge in Waldport, Oregon, replaced a deteriorating predecessor. HNTB was able to upgrade the bridge's size and capacity and, at the same time, create an aesthetically pleasing design.

Below: Environmental considerations such as vibration and noise were among the challenges facing HNTB architects for the addition of surgical suites at St. Cabrini Hospital. Built atop a preexisting parking structure, the Columbus Pavilion was a remarkable success for the architects.

With the goal of reducing traffic congestion along a segment of I-5 through Seattle, HNTB transportation engineers designed high-occupancy vehicle lanes to move more people in fewer vehicles.

built a library of planning, architectural, and engineering software, including many innovations developed by its professionals. A major element of the firm's total capability is a state-of-the-art computer-aided design and drafting (CADD) system. HNTB has a fully integrated digital network linking its design offices nationwide.

Today's engineering professionals must also excel as communicators. Presentations must be made in public forums, explaining the specific problems and alternatives of infrastructure projects and pointing out the advantages of each alternative to every identifiable segment of the community. Some of HNTB's successful communication approaches for community awareness and feedback have

included attitude surveys, workshops and group meetings, explanatory slide shows, films and videos, brochures and newsletters, and closed-circuit public-access TV programs.

HNTB encourages its employees to become active in the community, and many donate their expertise to local boards and organizations. Nationally, HNTB sponsors a Leaders program that recognizes employees for community involvement.

The Bellevue Transit Center was the first facility of its type in the region. HNTB provided transportation planning, urban design, preliminary and final architectural engineering design, and construction administration.

Competition for engineering, architecture, and planning services is keen. HNTB competes with a variety of national companies on local projects, and the Bellevue office can provide, or at least has access to providing, almost any service needed. One of the goals of the Bellevue office is to increase its market share of architecture services.

HNTB has found a home in the Bellevue community. The company came to the area for one purpose: to work on routing I-5 through Seattle and making connections to I-90. The project took 20 years to complete, and in the meantime, HNTB has successfully established itself. Today the office provides services in architecture, aviation, bridges and tunnels, construction, environmental engineering, industrial, transportation, and urban and regional planning.

Since 1954 HNTB has been active in bringing the latest developments in data processing to the engineering and design practices of the firm. The company has

CH2M HILL

Left: The improvements to Bellevue's N.E. Fourth Street designed by CH2M HILL provide increased capacity for vehicles, connect with a new freeway interchange, and also serve pedestrian needs in a growing, changing downtown core.

Below: CH2M HILL provides detailed stream flow and water-quality assessments for wastewater treatment, water supply, urban runoff, and other projects involving streams.

CH2M HILL first made its presence known in the Puget Sound region with a five-person office in 1960. Since then the company has become the largest engineering consulting firm in Washington and one of Bellevue's largest employers, paralleling the impressive growth and development of the region and the Eastside.

The small beginnings were similar to the beginnings of the worldwide CH2M HILL firm nearly 15 years earlier. The first employees were a college professor and three of his former students. They started it all in a room over a hardware store in Corvallis, Oregon, in 1946, and the organization now employs more than 4,000 people worldwide and operates from four districts that oversee offices in more than 55 cities nationwide and abroad.

The firm's name has been a curiosity since it was adopted in the 1950s. No one remembers exactly how the name CH2M evolved, but it represents the first initial of the last name of the four founders: Holly Cornell, Jim Howland, Burke Hayes, and Fred Merryfield. Years later the company merged with Clair A. Hill and Associates and the name became CH2M HILL.

One of the firm's founding partners, Holly Cornell, opened the Seattle regional office. The next Seattle regional manager, James Poirot, moved the office to Bellevue for the convenience of his employees. He is now chairman of worldwide CH2M HILL.

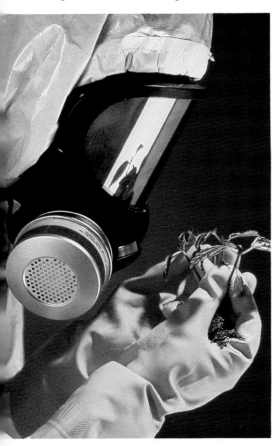

CH2M HILL is a leader in environmental restoration and waste site cleanup.

C.V. "Tom" Gibbs, who headed the regional office from 1983 to 1988 and is now senior vice-president of the firm, manages the northwest district and is a member of the company's board of directors. The northwest district includes Oregon, Alaska, Hawaii, and Washington. Following Gibbs as head of the Seattle region in 1988 was William Winter, one of the highly trained young leaders on whose shoulders the firm's future rests.

CH2M HILL has had a hand in many of the state's engineering success stories, some of which have changed the complexion of the region. One of the first major projects in the region was in 1966 for the Boeing Company, which asked CH2M HILL to participate in the design of its 432-acre aerospace center near Kent. Since those early years the firm has become a major contributor to environmental quality, especially work to preserve the quality of Puget Sound waters. One of the organization's largest single contracts is as the lead firm of a team of consultants designing the West Point sewage treatment plant. West Point is managed and operated by Metro, the agency responsible for sewage treatment for much of the greater Seattle area.

By the early 1970s CH2M HILL's engineers, planners, economists, and scientists were working on projects nationwide and internationally. Today the Seattle regional office is in downtown Bellevue where more than 400 employees work in a variety of engineering and environmental disciplines. Water and wastewater projects have long been a staple of the company's services. The firm's expertise is also recognized by private business and public agencies in solid and hazardous waste, civil engineering, transportation, agriculture, air quality, energy, and environmental services. Within each discipline, study and design services are complemented by capabilities in economics, urban and regional planning, natural sciences, and construction management. The regional office also serves its statewide clients from area offices in Yakima, Richland, and Spokane.

CH2M HILL is employee-owned, providing a sense of pride in the organization. This makes for business culture that is oriented to people and rests on the belief that employees who are committed to their jobs will do quality work.

The latest computer technology is available to the firm's design staff.

For more than 25 years CH2M HILL has helped public and private utilities, municipalities, industries, and developers with environmental investigations and solutions.

However, CH2M HILL does more than provide professional services to the communities it serves. A community involvement spirit is an integral part of the firm's business philosophy and results in many employees being involved in activities that benefit area citizens and organizations.

In response to the region's most pressing challenge, CH2M HILL has devoted considerable effort to transportation needs and solutions. Two of the most recognized contributions are the N.E. Fourth Street improvement project for the City of Bellevue and the City of Renton's Oakesdale Avenue project, featuring a six-lane bridge on Interstate 405 with a five-lane arterial passing under it.

The Bellevue project is an excellent example of how CH2M HILL design work is a part of providing solutions to problems resulting from the area's rapid growth. In addition to providing Bellevue with a widened street from the city's downtown park to a new I-405 interchange, the Fourth Street project emphasizes pedestrian amenities. CH2M HILL's design concepts include wider sidewalks, trees to buffer pedestrians from traffic, benches, and landscaping. Both the Bellevue and Renton projects required extraordinary teamwork in working closely with a number of governmental bodies and agencies. On the Oakesdale project, team members included the City of Renton, the State of Washington, various contractors, and the Soil and Conservation Service. A similar mixture of governmental bodies was involved on the N.E. Fourth Street project.

CH2M HILL takes justifiable pride in anticipating the region's significant issues—solid waste, hazardous and toxic waste, transportation, and water pollution—and providing services designed to make the region a more livable place. But while the firm is involved in the large issues and projects, it continues to provide valuable services to businesses and to governmental bodies of all sizes. The company's commitment to the region encompasses involvement by employees and the firm in helping make the Pacific Northwest an attractive and prosperous place to live, work, and play.

SDL CORPORATION

SDL Corporation has built its entire organization around understanding the needs of real estate developers. Since the company was formed in 1977, SDL's understanding of the development process has become finely honed. The company has worked with some of the best developers in the area on some of the most highly regarded projects in the area.

SDL president Dave Lowry thinks the firm's success is due to some basic strategies: employing people who know how to get the job done and know how to do it competitively; applying innovative solutions that come from solid construction industry experience; realizing the importance of marketing a project, not just building it; and thinking like a developer, not just a contractor.

"We approach each assignment as a unique project, tailoring our methods to fit the project's special needs and challenges," says Lowry. "Our strength comes from our broad experience with different building types, since we've worked on projects as varied as office buildings, hotels, and medical

Newport Tower, a mid-rise building with challenging environmental considerations, is just one of SDL's many successful projects.

labs. We know how to anticipate problems that can jeopardize a job."

SDL is a full-service general contractor that is dedicated to providing quality construction for office buildings, business parks, warehouses and distribution facilities, hotels, and retail centers. The company has built some of Puget Sound's most noted projects and has gained a reputation as a general contractor that approaches each assignment as a unique project. "We maintain exceptionally tight control over the construction on each job," Lowry states.

SDL has built a lot of new projects, but it also has been associated with the remodeling and refurbishing of many local projects, including the Court in the Square project that involved renovation of two turn-of-the-century warehouses and the construction of a glass atrium between them. SDL handled the dramatic Tower Building facelift that brought this well-known landmark up to contemporary standards of design excellence and appearance.

The company also specializes in interior construction and finish work. SDL has completed tenant improvements for Westcoast Hotels, Thai Airways, and BA Mortgage, and has worked extensively at

Corporate Campus East, recipient of two prestigious design awards, is built of site precast concrete and encompasses more than 300,000 square feet.

1201 Third Avenue.

Lowry attributes the firm's success to its reputation of paying attention to detail as well as to team effort. In the 14 years SDL has been in business, it has grown to become the fifth-largest general contractor in the region, with revenues exceeding $85 million in 1988.

SDL employs some 55 people at its Bellevue headquarters and effects a work force of up to 700 people per year at its peak season. The company currently handles some 15 projects—large and small—each year. SDL's volume increased by 30 percent from 1986 to 1987, and doubled from 1987 to 1988.

Despite the accolades, Lowry claims the firm will not duplicate this growth over the next few years. "We have gained our market share on a foundation of quali-

Despite the phenomenal growth SDL Corporation's management still holds strong to the philosophy that it must give back to the community in which it thrives. Lowry and his management team are active construction industry and community leaders. The firm is an active member of the Bellevue Chamber of Commerce and the Bellevue Downtown Association. Lowry's pet projects are the Boys and Girls Club in Kirkland and the Eastside Boy Scouts of America. The company is actively involved in issues and concerns of the construction industry through involvement with the Associated General Contractors of Washington.

"It may sound trite," says Lowry, "but we feel like this community has been good to us and we owe it to serve."

ty," he says. "We are committed to delivering this quality, and we will never sacrifice it for growth."

SDL is sensitive to a developer's strategies, and the company's expertise in project management has strengthened its reputation.

Yet SDL's management is not afraid to tackle the most difficult projects. Newport Tower's geographical considerations alone made it a difficult project to get under way. The $11-million, 285,000-square-foot, Class A mid-rise provided several challenges, including environmental constraints that delayed construction, making its schedule sensitive since the day ground was broken. But SDL was able to find cost-effective solutions that made it an economically viable project.

SDL has significantly contributed to Bellevue's growth. The company has built such local landmarks as the Corporate Campus East, the Crossroads, and the Vernon Publications building, to name a few.

Above: Seattle's Broadway Market features a large, well-lit atrium that recalls the ambience of a European-style open-air market. SDL helped to preserve the spirit of this festive retail facility.

Right: Kennedy Associates of Seattle benefited from the remodeling expertise of the SDL team.

Below: Duwamish Office Park, a dramatic structure in Seattle, demonstrates SDL Corporation's diversity and versatility.

LEASE CRUTCHER LEWIS

With the dramatic growth of industrial and commercial interests in the Northwest, one company has come to symbolize excellence in construction for the region: Lease Crutcher Lewis. Throughout Washington, Oregon, and Alaska, the company has produced landmark projects of quality and innovation. Beginning with such milestones as the completion of the first passenger terminal at Seattle Tacoma Airport, Lease Crutcher Lewis has filled its history with achievements that have not only accommodated the area's development, but pioneered advanced construction techniques to make the Northwest the leader in many high-tech commercial fields.

As the technology boom

brings this sector's industry into the national spotlight, Lease Crutcher Lewis has been instrumental in providing the facilities necessary to support these rapid advances. Computer management and commercial aircraft production buildings have been completed for the Boeing Company. Specialized instrument manufacturing plants were produced for Hewlett-Packard. Pacific Northwest Bell and General Telephone both selected the company to construct their regional headquarters. Not surprisingly, the ultra-dynamic superconductor industry has chosen Lease Crutcher Lewis to aid its efforts as well, with the completion of National Semiconductor's "clean room" laboratories, which are vital to the manufacturing process. As the Northwest's role in the nation's technology has increased, so has Lease Crutcher Lewis' commitment to state-of-the-art building production.

The company's commercial sector projects have set the standard for the region. Weyerhaeuser's air transportation facilities and Security Pacific's operations center are two outstanding examples of Lease Crutcher Lewis' capacity to meet the needs of corporate expansion. Yet perhaps the most spectac-

ular monument to the company's expertise is The Salish Lodge at Snoqualmie Falls. This 91-room masterpiece has become the premier resort in all of Washington State, with the 270-foot falls being complemented beautifully by the natural wood styling of the lodge. The project, which was completed on a fast-track production schedule, stands as a lasting contribution to the state's tourism and economy. In honor of this extraordinary accomplishment, the Pacific Coast Builder Conference presented Lease Crutcher Lewis the 1988 Golden Nugget Award for Hotels and Resorts.

As the Northwest experiences one of the country's highest growth rates, the need for capable, forward-thinking companies is self-evident. Lease Crutcher Lewis' proven ability to deliver quality and performance has made it one of the foremost leaders in the construction industry. The Associated General Contractors chose Lease Crutcher Lewis to construct its Washington State headquarters, a fitting testimony to the company's reputation among its clients and

This biomedical research laboratory facility was completed in only six months. The design, by The Callison Partnership, features underground parking and is located on a "tight site," where there was little space for work.

its peers. For the competition of today and the challenges of the future, Lease Crutcher Lewis will continue the excellence it has demonstrated for more than 100 years.

Facing page, top: The Salish Lodge provided immense challenges to the skill of Lease Crutcher Lewis. Construction was completed during the inclement winter months in a considerably short amount of time. Owned by Puget Western and designed by Mithun Partners, the lodge overlooks the 270-foot Snoqualmie Falls.

Facing page, bottom: Lease Crutcher Lewis' complete renovation and addition to General Telephone Northwest's headquarters did not interfere with the company's operations. The project was designed by The Callison Partnership.

Right: The Virginia Mason Clinic was built by Lease Crutcher Lewis on a fast-track schedule to take advantage of dry weather. The 70,000-square-foot clinic was designed by Mahlum and Nodfors.

MITHUN PARTNERS

In 1949 a University of Washington professor of architecture decided to establish his own firm in an effort to parallel and complement his academic career. Teaching was a lifelong commitment for Omer Mithun, but he needed to implement the concepts of the classroom.

Throughout the years that followed, Mithun Partners underwent a number of evolutions. Former students joined the staff. In the early 1950s another Bellevue architect asked Mithun to join him in a move to Seattle. Mithun declined, preferring to stay "where my heart is"—in Bellevue.

Early Mithun projects were primarily residential. As the Bellevue area diversified and matured, so, too, did the scope of Mithun projects. Design work created churches, banks, shopping centers, medical clinics, office buildings, city halls, and fire stations for the citizens of the area.

Omer Mithun became active in the Bellevue community. The first chairman of the Bellevue Planning Commission, he served that group for more than 19 years. Shortly before his death in 1983, a

feature article in the *Journal-American* dubbed him "Mr. Architect," crediting Mithun with giving the Eastside "buildings that belong" and his firm with influencing the best of Bellevue designs.

Today Mithun Partners is a firm of architects and interior designers nationally recognized for excellence, with projects throughout the western United States. Its dedication to appropriate design has resulted in enduring architecture that performs functionally and aesthetically, enhancing each community it enters. Of equal importance is its commitment to clients, its dedication to bringing a satisfactory return to developers, and the added value over the lifetime of each project.

Mithun Partners is widely respected for such projects as the award-winning Fairwood Library in Renton; Koll Center-Canyon Park in the Technology Corridor of Bothell; Pierpointe Condominiums on the Kirkland waterfront; Plaza Port West Shopping Center in Ketchican, Alaska; and Orange Tree Resort and Conference Center in Scottsdale, Arizona. Its interior design staff brings a strong background in hospitality design while responding to the design, space planning, and purchasing needs of other Mithun clients in unique and appropriate ways.

Mithun Partners offices are a

Mithun Partners designed downtown Bellevue's Pacific First Plaza with eight corner offices on each floor, maximizing views of the mountains and Lake Washington. The development also offers extensive office and retail space. Photo by Robert Pisano

catalyst for creativity. More than 50 employees bring individual artistry to their problem-solving design teams to produce buildings that serve both client and community goals.

The strength of Mithun lies in the symbiotic energies of its management team. Chairman Don Bowman, with the company for more than 25 years and a Fellow of the American Institute of Architects, is a motivator of people. He constantly stimulates his employees' creativity; through exemplary design and gentle suggestion he encourages staff to be the best it can be. An acknowledged leader in his profession (1988-1989 president of the Seattle chapter of the AIA), president Thom Emrich provides Mithun leadership in both design and organizational areas. Committed to the integration of

Cascading decks and formal courtyard plazas join lawn areas, streamside retreats, and jogging trails to create a relaxing campus environment at Bellevue's Corporate Campus East, designed by Mithun Partners. Photo by Charles Pearson

computers into the design field, his is a leading voice championing Mithun's goal of providing a computer for every workstation.

Mithun's success does not stem from the examples set by these two alone. The firm's management team of principals and associates is committed to providing a superior product for each client. It is through the collective efforts of well-chosen staff that Mithun has built its solid reputation and continues to thrive in its highly competitive field.

In recent years expanded commitment to developer-oriented projects has deepened Mithun's impact on retail and corporate park design. Spearheaded by vice-president Vince Ferrese, Mithun offers clients the ability to control costs and project schedules so vital in this market. In 1987 Ferrese's remodel and second-story addition to the JCPenney-Tacoma store won first place in *Chain Store Age Executive*'s New Store of the Year Competition.

Vice-president Jerry Cichanski brings to the firm design excellence and a flair for the unexpected. At his suggestion the concept of the Mithun study tour abroad was born. In October 1988, 20 staff members traveled to London in the first of a series of educa-

The historic Salish Lodge at Snoqualmie Falls (above), expanded and remodeled by Mithun Partners, includes 91 guest rooms (each with Jacuzzi and fireplace), an expansive dining room, a lounge, a library, meeting/ banquet rooms, and a country store. Intimate rooms, a warm Northwest-style design, and a "country inn" tradition have made the lodge a success. Photo by Dick Busher

Above right: The steep site and adjacent 270-foot waterfall required an innovative design that disguises the size of the 61,000-square-foot facility. Photo by Gregg Krogstad.

tion tours beyond the United States. With broadened design perspectives, fresh points of view, and a renewed spirit of camaraderie, the Mithun team returned eager to apply lessons learned to appropriate future client needs.

Other activity expanding the company's design horizon is Mithun's work in Japan. From public housing in Kobe to resort condominiums on the flanks of Mount Fuji, its projects serve to demonstrate American housing designs and construction. Not only have American building materials and techniques been imported, but concepts of neighborhood planning as well.

Kobe, Japan, is a long way from Bellevue, Washington—yet Mithun approaches both communities with an affinity to careful site

and market development. Over its 40-year history the firm has won hundreds of awards for its work. Many are due to the design and planning talents of vice-president Bill Kreager, director of residential design and frequent leader of national seminars on residential design and site planning.

Mithun architects are involved in the communities in which they live. A Bellevue resident for more than 38 years, Don Bowman has dedicated thousands of hours to the downtown Bellevue development plan, a process highly gratifying in the stunningly telescoped interval between plan and execution in this uniquely developing city.

Mithun Partners is looking to the future. As practicing professionals, national speakers, university instructors, and award jurors on the subject of architecture, the firm's employees are in touch with the ever-changing needs of society and its built environment. The company's history of community involvement provides an ongoing impetus to create projects that complement the fabric of the communities in which they are situated. Mithun Partners views this ongoing interaction with communities as a mutually enriching relationship, giving it fresh and ever-expanding perspectives on architecture and its place in the human experience.

WILSEY & HAM PACIFIC, INC.

Almost hidden in a tree-thick alcove off 112th Avenue N.E., the corporate offices of Wilsey & Ham Pacific reflect the firm's sensitivity to land and the environment. The planning, engineering, surveying, and landscape design company has applied this sensitivity to some of the region's best-known projects.

Earl P. Wilsey and Lee Ham founded the business in 1942 in Foster City, California. In 1968 Wilsey & Ham opened an office in Renton to work on the Forward Thrust Project, a million-dollar construction project for a City of Seattle sewer separation system. In 1972 the company obtained the Mill Creek project. From that point, Wilsey & Ham was established in the region. By 1988 the firm had offices in Foster City, Portland, and Bellevue.

Early in 1988 Wilsey & Ham's president resigned, and Jeff Daggett, from the Bellevue office, was named president. Daggett was instrumental in structuring a buy-out by the offices in Portland and Bellevue, which are now known as Wilsey & Ham Pacific. Although it has been in business for only a year, the new company offers some 47 years of experience.

Unlike engineering firms that specialize in a specific discipline, Wilsey & Ham Pacific takes an integrated approach to projects and works as a complete design team. The group can handle most any design problem outside of the building, including infrastructure planning and improvement, land improvement, environmental impact studies, and land-use studies.

The Mill Creek project has brought the firm prominence. Wilsey & Ham Pacific began when the land was filled with trees. The firm handled all the planning and infrastructure development of this master-planned community, which is often cited as an example of how land should be sensitively developed.

Another example of the firm's work can be seen in the recently completed Bellevue Place. Wilsey & Ham Pacific did the environmental impact statement, all the traffic studies, and all the civil engineering work and surveying on the water, sewer, street, and sidewalk design.

The firm has handled a variety of civil engineering projects for Microsoft, and it has completed many local road projects, including work on

Wilsey & Ham Pacific, Inc., provided the planning, surveying, and infrastructure design for Mill Creek, a master-planned community that is now home to more than 11,000 people.

Northeast Eighth Street, Northup Way, and portions of the I-90 highway. More than 30 percent of the firm's business comes from counties or municipalities.

Wilsey & Ham Pacific has developed a reputation for its parks work and has been recognized for its landscape design achievements and environmental excellence by the American Society of Landscape Architects, the Washington Roadside Council, and the Washington State Department of Ecology.

The firm has perfected its presentation techniques with the aid of computer-enhanced graphics, which enable clients to visually assess what a particular development will look like and understand how their property will be affected.

Wilsey & Ham Pacific, Inc., staff and principals are involved in several technical and professional organizations and in community organizations, including the Bellevue Downtown Association, the Bellevue Rotary, the Transportation Management Association, and the Bellevue Chamber of Commerce.

Clients of Wilsey & Ham Pacific, Inc., benefit from the firm's computer-generated perspectives of design projects. Shown is an emergency vehicle operating course designed for the Washington State Patrol.

Photo by Gary Greene

12
QUALITY OF LIFE

Medical and educational institutions contribute to the quality of life for Eastside residents.

Photo by Gary Greene

OVERLAKE HOSPITAL MEDICAL CENTER

Overlake Hospital Medical Center is among the Eastside's proudest accomplishments. Since the day it opened with 52 beds in 1960, the hospital has been in a constant state of renovation and expansion, while still providing conscientious, quality medical care. The hospital's staff and board of trustees invariably are querying the community's health care needs and shaping the hospital's operations to answer those needs.

Overlake Hospital Medical Center is a shining example of public/private cooperation. The facility is still run by a 17-member board of trustees comprised of Eastside citizens who volunteer their time, talents, and energy to shape the hospital's policies and financial future. Employing some 1,300 full- and part-time nurses, technicians, and managerial and support staff, the 235-bed hospital is well poised to offer distinctive medical care. There are more than 400 board-certified physicians on the hospital staff.

Approximately 15,000 patients were admitted to the facility in 1988, and more than 27,000 patients are treated annually in Over-

With more than 400 board-certified physicians and 1,300 additional employees, Overlake Hospital Medical Center is well prepared to serve the medical needs of Eastside residents.

lake's Emergency Department and Trauma Center. A small community hospital in the 1960s, Overlake is now the major medical center in one of the state's fastest growing metropolitan areas. A "people helping people" attitude is deeply rooted among the hospital's physicians, nurses, staff, and volunteers.

Overlake Hospital Medical Center is considered an asset to

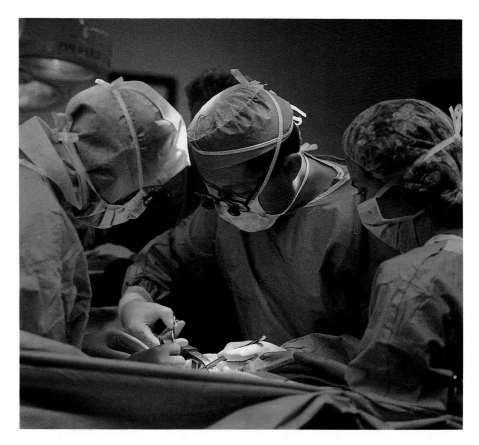

Overlake's nationally recognized surgical staff is dedicated to the success of each operation.

the growth and continuing viability of the community. The hospital has proven to be the community resource its founders dreamed about when they united to build the facility back in the early 1950s. The history of Overlake Hospital Medical Center is a fascinating example of what can be done when people care about each other and the community in which they live.

Back in 1953 Bellevue's one traffic light adequately accommodated the traffic of the town's 4,000 citizens. But if a resident had to be hospitalized, he had to go into Seattle. Newspaper accounts of emergency runs across the lake told of residents narrowly escaping death and some even dying because they could not get urgent medical attention. A rash of these incidents alarmed citizens; soon the entire community decided it wanted—it desperately needed—a

Each year Overlake's comfortable lobby greets thousands of patients who have come to expect quality, conscientious medical care. Photo (right) by Roger Turk

tal. Many call FitzGerald a pillar of the hospital. Auxiliary member Lorraine Weltzein was—and still is—a cheerleader for the hospital, rallying the community to support the institution's opening. Scores of community leaders and business executives contributed hours of energy and expertise to the cause.

After seven years of fund raising, matched with Hill-Burton grants from the federal government, ground was broken in 1958. The week before the hospital opened, auxiliary members donned aprons and gathered mops, brooms, and dust cloths to clean the brand-new building; demonstrating the spirit of the community.

This same spirit is prevalent today. The community's investment has come full circle, and Over-

community hospital.

Overlake Memorial Hospital Association incorporated as a not-for-profit group, and immediately it began raising funds. It was a grass-roots effort, virtually every resident was involved in raising money to build the hospital. Early on, local women's groups became the backbone of the effort. These groups, known as auxiliaries, hosted teas, dances, art shows, theater productions, and golf tournaments. These ladies even solicited door to door. The Fabiola Auxiliary was the first of the eight auxiliaries that continue to volunteer for the hospital.

The business sector was vigorously involved in making the hospital a reality. The property on which the hospital sits was donated by local businesspeople and physicians. Frederick and Nelson's department store in Bellevue Square donated proceeds from its day care center to the hospital

fund. Owners of the Candy Cane Kitchen, a local diner, placed a jar at the cash register and insisted customers drop in loose change before leaving.

Shortly before the hospital opened, a $25,000 deficit was revealed. Board trustees actually signed personal notes to come up with the needed funding. Edward FitzGerald, the first president of the board of trustees, helped raise thousands of dollars for the hospi-

lake Hospital Medical Center is a resource for all Eastside residents. As a not-for-profit, non-tax-supported hospital, Overlake has reinvested the fees it receives for patient care into expanding services and upgrading medical facilities. Yet Overlake Hospital Medical Center is available to anyone in the community, regardless of his or her ability to pay. In 1988 nearly one million dollars of the hospital's services went to charity care.

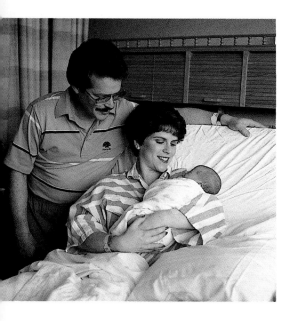

New families enjoy the assurance of Overlake's expert care in family-oriented obstetrics, in fertility, laser surgery, and neonatology.

Through keen financial management, strict operating guidelines, and philanthropic support, expansion plans have been on the drawing table and in progress literally since the facility opened.

During the early 1960s Overlake patients needing highly specialized care still had to be referred to Seattle hospitals. As the community grew, demand for a wide range of medical care heightened. As each need was assessed, the hospital and its core of volunteers took action. The institution has garnered national recognition for its specialized care: a highly sophisticated surgical facility, an open-heart surgery program, a nationally recognized critical care facility, a state-of-the-art emergency and trauma center, full-service diagnostic and therapeutic services, inpatient psychiatric care, cancer care, an education conference center, and a Birthing Center where more than 2,000 babies are born each year.

Overlake has developed a highly recognized surgical facility and is equipped for specialized procedures, including ophthalmologic, otologic, orthopedic, plastic, gynecologic, urologic, cardiac, and neurosurgery, as well as general procedures.

Prior to July 1987 patients diag-nosed as needing open-heart surgery still had to go to a Seattle hospital. Today Eastside residents requiring open-heart surgery, as well as complex cardiac catheterization procedures, can be treated and recover at Overlake. Physicians and staff had estimated they would perform some 300 open-heart procedures during the first two years; more than 500 were performed. The success of the open-heart program is evident in a mortality rate that is lower than the national average.

In 1987 the Overlake Outpatient Surgery Center opened, coupling modern technology and a caring medical staff. Eastside residents may receive the best in short-term surgical care at the facility that has gained national notoriety for its "patient-friendly" design. The center is comprised of four surgical suites and two recovery rooms. Surgeries performed on an outpatient basis include minor urological procedures; ear, nose, and throat procedures; biopsies; gynecological procedures; and orthopedic procedures such as arthroscopies.

Overlake's new Surgical Pavilion is scheduled for completion during 1989. Several millon dollars worth of leading-edge medical equipment and state-of-the art surgery suites will enhance the efforts of the highly specialized nursing and physician staffs in ICU and CCU. The critical care staffs are known for their progressive team approach to treating serious and life-threatening medical problems. A new Medical Imaging Department also will be housed in the Surgical Pavilion.

The Emergency Department and Trauma Center at Overlake provides top-notch emergency care—from the most minor medical emergencies to those that require life-support care on a moment's notice. The emergency room staff works closely with the Bellevue Fire Department's Medic One team, which is based at Overlake. Medic One paramedics have received national recognition for their extraordinarily high success rate for resuscitating patients.

Medical Imaging services, including radiology, computerized tomography scanning, ultrasound, nuclear medicine, echocardiography, pathology, histology, and others, are available at Overlake Hospital. Both inpatients and outpatients may receive on-site therapeutic services, including physical, occupational, and speech therapy, as well as rehabilitation medicine and radiation cancer treatment.

Overlake's psychiatric program is the only facility of its kind on the Eastside and offers one of the few volunteer psychiatric units in the area. The program provides comprehensive care for each patient. Treatment methods include individual and group therapy, medicines, and family support and involvement.

Overlake's Cancer Care Team—physicians, dietitians, nurses, physical therapists, and social workers—gather weekly to discuss the progress of each cancer patient and to design treatment plans. The 16-bed Richard E. Lange Oncology Unit provides cancer patients and their families

Overlake's commitment to providing diagnostic technology is demonstrated in the hospital's Medical Imaging Department. Photos by Doug Plummer

with a sense of continuity and relaxation. Various support groups are available as well.

The Birthing Center provides a warm, homey atmosphere for new families. Seven hotel-like LDR (labor/delivery/recovery) rooms allow a woman to labor, deliver, and recover in the same room. Separate delivery rooms for high-risk mothers are also available if needed. Overlake is becoming a leader in the Northwest in family-oriented obstetrics, infertility, laser surgery, and neonatology. A Level II, high-risk nursery accommodates premature and critically ill infants; more than 160 premature and high-risk babies are treated yearly in the Special Care nursery. A parenting information line provides information about pregnancy, childbirth, and parenting. The Stork Club, a five-year membership program for mothers who deliver at the hospital, provides

benefits to families during and after pregnancy, including discounts at area stores, a newsletter, nutritional information, and family activities.

Simply stated, Overlake's commitment to community health education is unparalleled in the Puget Sound area. The education conference center is a community facility that houses four meeting rooms, the Edward M. FitzGerald Auditorium, and a system of high-quality audiovisual equipment. Classes, seminars, and other health education activities are open to residents year round. National and local experts lead discussions and workshops about such topics as child rearing, nutrition, exercise, stress reduction, and senior citizen life-style.

Overlake Hospital Medical Center's future appears optimistic as it positions itself for the twenty-first century. Overlake's goal of providing affordable, accessible, high-quality health care has earned it an excellent reputation as a full-service health care resource to the greater Eastside community.

Who We Are
We are a not-for-profit, non-tax-supported community hospital offering, in association with our medical staff, a broad range of carefully selected health technologies and specialty services that are provided with efficiency and sensitivity to patient needs and preferences.

Why We Are
We are dedicated to enhancing the quality of life on the Eastside by maintaining and improving people's health through a partnership that encourages healthy life-styles and provides appropriate health services.

How We Work
We strive to provide quality service in a businesslike manner, to be a good employer, competitive, financially viable, and a responsible corporate citizen. Our operating principles are to: provide value to our patients and their families; act with respect and sensitivity toward the individual; function with integrity; encourage excellence, professionalism, and innovation; and operate with financial responsibility.

BELLEVUE COMMUNITY COLLEGE

To see it from the road, Bellevue Community College might appear to be a sleepy college campus in a pleasant neighborhood, set away from the traffic by a small forest. But appearances can be deceiving.

Bellevue Community College is an active, integral part of the area. It provides students with freshman- and sophomore-level education that half of the total student body carries on to a four-year school. It offers area residents training in 19 occupations. It acts as an educational resource for the business community by providing specialized classes for specific companies at their request.

Community members can take a continuing education class for personal enjoyment or professional enrichment. People with special needs can find help with reading, writing, and mathematics; guidance through life transitions such as divorce, separation, or wid-

A western view down Landerholm Circle, the major entrance to the college. Landerholm Circle is named after Merle E. Landerholm, the first president of the college. Photo by Valerie Chapman

owhood; and assistance for personal success.

It does all this, and more, with a flair—at least the 12,500 students who attend each quarter think so. Their numbers make the college the second-largest single-campus college in western Washington.

BCC has a commitment to create educated students—not those who are merely trained—because local business leaders have indicated that students who can communicate, reason, solve problems, and interact well with others make better employees than those who can simply accomplish a task. All students, whether they concentrate on an academic program or an occupational one, are graduated with strong communication, reasoning, and interpersonal skills.

In addition to required course work, students have the opportunity to participate in learning communities, or interdisciplinary programs. Each program is one-quarter of three disciplines taught on one subject, to equal a full class load for the term. For example, one class from arts and humanities, one from social science, and one from science will be joined under a common theme, giving the participant college credit for all three subjects—credit that can be transferred to a four-year school.

Occupational programs can be completed in two years, except for interior design. Detailed courses and two off-campus practicums require three years of those students. The program was extended at the request of industry advisers who suggested that the extra work would give graduates a

All 108 acres of the gently rolling, wooded campus are fully accessible. Photo by Valerie Chapman

special edge in the job market.

In fact, businesspeople and community leaders advise the college in many areas of operation, from occupational programs to the selection of the president and trustees. In turn, college administrators and faculty participate in community and business activities by serving committees in the community and with the chamber of commerce.

BCC's leaders strongly believe that a partnership between the business community and the college benefits both and, because the college has a firm commitment to lifelong learning, the administrators in the Continuing Education Division have particularly strong ties to the business community. The division offers a large number of work-related classes spanning a variety of skills and practices that

Above: Individual instruction is a hallmark of BCC's commitment to its students. Photo by Valerie Chapman

Right: The Human Development Center provides academic, career, and personal counseling to BCC's 13,000 students. Photo by Karen Smaalders

are in demand by business owners, managers, and office workers. Many of these classes are developed because businesspeople have made their needs known.

Other classes are developed specifically for particular businesses for their employees and attended exclusively by their employees. The college works in a similar fashion with the chamber of commerce, developing seminars and workshops for chamber members on topics such as customer service, marketing, and business growth and planning.

Other business/college partnerships deal with foreign trade, especially with Pacific Rim countries. The relationship with foreign countries also includes the English Language Institute, which offers intensive English language classes to foreign nationals.

But a college is more than classes. Special services help students achieve success, and extracurricular activities give students an opportunity to broaden their experiences.

Special Services counseling helps minority, disabled, and disadvantaged students achieve academic success. Displaced homemakers and other women in transition can get personal help,

legal referrals, and special skills training through the Women's Resource Center. Academic advising, career information, and specific help for success in college is available in the Human Development Center. BCC is also one of the few community colleges in the state that offers health services.

To enhance their learning, students may participate in intercollegiate athletics; music, drama, and dance performances; Phi Theta Kappa honorary society; *The Advocate* student newspaper; KBCS-FM community radio station, student government; Telos senior citizens program; and a literary magazine.

About 950 faculty, classified staff, hourly staff, full- and part-time faculty, and administrators operate the college, which has an $18.3-million budget. The 108-acre campus includes a planetarium, gymnasium, performing arts theater, athletic track and field, fitness center, conference rooms,

cable TV station, and child care facilities—and, of course, all those trees.

"Community" is the key word in BCC's name. Being an active participant in the community is vital to Bellevue Community College's success as an educational institution.

In 1989 BCC awarded degrees to nearly 800 students—the largest graduating class in the school's history. Photo by Valerie Chapman

LAKE WASHINGTON VOCATIONAL TECHNICAL INSTITUTE

Many people who live in the Puget Sound region have never set foot on the immense 56-acre campus of the Lake Washington Vocational Technical Institute in Kirkland. They don't know what they're missing.

Literally an entire training city under one roof, the facility has more than 200,000 square feet (4.5 acres) devoted to job preparation and training. Behind the sleek, modern structure, the institute buzzes night and day with more than 23,000 students registered each year.

Serving one of the fastest-growing job markets in the United States, Lake Washington VocTech is accredited by the Northwest Association of Schools and Colleges, and its 43 training programs are approved by the Superintendent of Public Instruction for Washington

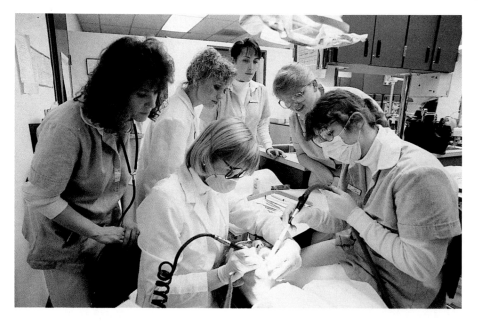

Students in VocTech's dental assisting program observe a dentist at the school's dental lab.

State. The publicly funded postsecondary institution was established and authorized under Washington State law and is committed to preparing people for jobs and upgrading the skills of those already employed.

Students, whose ages range from 16 to the mid-60s, can focus on a specific career field by developing job skills in their areas of primary interest. Students are also exposed to other courses related to their programs that might help them build a broader base of opportunity as their careers unfold. More important, students at the VocTech learn exactly what local employers tell the school's administrators they want and need from employees.

What can students of Lake Washington VocTech expect from their education? First, they can expect to receive the highest-quality instruction from a deeply involved staff, 85 percent of whom have worked in the industry they teach. Second, students can expect to get a job upon graduation. Approximately 93 percent of the school's students find work in the specific field in which they trained within 90 days of completing their training.

Students at VocTech come from diverse backgrounds. Some are young adults working toward making it on their own. Some are veteran workers who have been laid off or are seeking a job

change. Some are women returning to the work force. Many have some college in their backgrounds, while others left high school and have returned to complete their diplomas or GEDs. Others are employees of firms that have arranged with VocTech to provide specific skills training. Boeing, USWest, Safeway, and Genie Industries are just some of the companies served in this way. Cooperative training is one of the strengths of the institute.

Regardless of their age, sex, or job status, students come to VocTech because they are motivated to create a better future for themselves. So what can a person learn at Lake Washington VocTech? One might start by taking advantage of the school's career guidance counseling. Students can take full- and part-time classes in accounting, automotive, bookkeeping, computers, construction, culinary arts, dental assistant, diesel, drafting, electronics, horticulture, hydraulics, insurance, landscaping, legal secretary, management, marketing, medical assistant, office skills, real estate, refrigeration, shorthand, surveying, technical illustration, teller, tenkey operation, typing, welding, and word processing, just to name a few.

An auto body technician student uses a unibody frame-straightening machine.

And if that's not enough, students can also take courses in personal finance, parenting, home improvement, cooking, and sewing. Still other classes offer the opportunity to learn and develop hobbies and interests for personal enrichment and extra income.

Full-time classes meet for 30 hours each week and emphasize realistic, hands-on training. Students who work are able to take advantage of VocTech's part-time classes. Some attend on a part-time basis to try out a new career they are interested in. Students with children appreciate the quality, on-site child-care program available.

Many students at Lake Washington VocTech receive financial aid to further their education. The institute participates in the Pell Grant, Supplemental Educational Opportunity Grant, Work Study, and the Washington Guaranteed Student Loan programs. The school is also approved for funding for veterans' benefits, the Division of Vocational Rehabilitation, the Department of Labor and Industries, and the Job Training Partnership Act.

With all this, why is it that Lake Washington Vocational Technical Institute is one of the region's best-kept secrets? Dr. Don W. Fowler, director, addresses this question daily, and he has a vision that five years from now, 10 out of 10 residents of the region

Taking advantage of the school's technological resources, a drafting student works with VocTech's computer-aided drafting (CAD) equipment.

will know of the school and will realize that its efforts are just as important as those of area community colleges and the University of Washington. How do Dr. Fowler and Lake Washington VocTech administrators plan to effect this vision? With vision. Dr. Fowler and his staff have prepared four long-range visions for the institution that address these goals. They are:

—Business, industry, and government will seek out Lake Washington VocTech and its graduates because of the quality of job training and retraining. The focus of these relationships will be economic development.

—Parents (families) of Eastside communities will see Lake Washington VocTech as an integral part of a kindergarten through postsecondary education system.

—Government agencies, organizations, and institutions that interface and contract with the education and training network in the Puget Sound region will see VocTech as a full partner in their network.

—Lake Washington VocTech will function as a lifelong education and learning center for the adult and family.

The institution's administrators realize these visions are a challenge. But progress already is apparent. Community awareness is higher than it has ever been since the school opened in 1949 as a postwar training facility.

Today more than 400 employers volunteer their time to serve on advisory committees. They meet regularly to fine tune and make changes to the curriculum, equipment, and instruction for each training program. It is this direct involvement of knowledgeable and dedicated citizens that ensures the vitality and longevity of the Lake Washington Vocational Technical Institute well into the twenty-first century.

The main mall area is a thoroughfare for 23,000 students, young and old, who enhance both their job skills and their lives at VocTech.

GROUP HEALTH COOPERATIVE OF PUGET SOUND

Group Health Cooperative of Puget Sound is the nation's largest consumer-governed health care organization and the Northwest's largest health maintenance organization (HMO). It provides prepaid health care to more than 430,000 people, 117,000 of whom are Eastside residents.

Group Health operates hospitals, specialty centers, family health centers, and a variety of other health care programs in communities statewide.

Group Health has been an active Puget Sound presence for more than 40 years. In 1947 Group Health succeeded in building a coalition of consumers, employees, and, employers willing to invest in the health care cooperative, as well as physicians who were committed to providing prepaid care as salaried staff members.

Group Health Cooperative began with 6,400 members. From 1969 to 1989 enrollment increased from 122,000 to more than 430,000, an annual growth rate of more than 12 percent. Today one out of every seven Puget Sound region residents belongs to Group Health, and approximately 80 percent of all enrollees have their premiums paid at least in part by their employers.

Group Health's medical staff is the fourth-largest prepaid group practice in the nation. The organization is the state's ninth-largest employer with an annual payroll of more than $166 million in 1988.

One indicator of the quality of its medical care is the fact that virtually all (99 percent) of the organization's physicians are board certified, having passed an exacting competency test. This compares to a nationwide average of 64 to 79 percent board certification. More than one-third of Group Health physicians have academic appointments at the University of Washington School of Medicine or other institutions.

Group Health manages

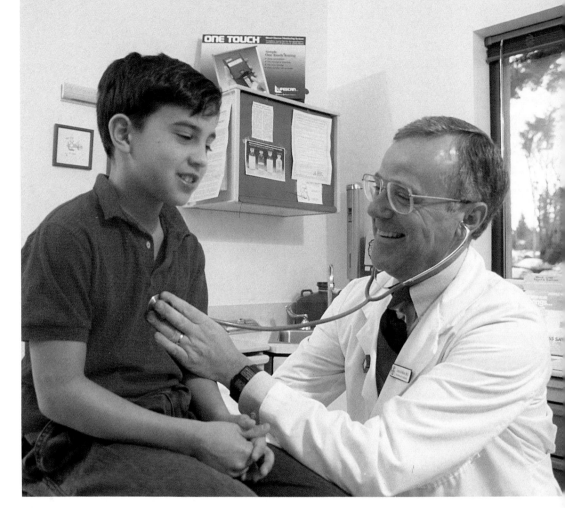

health care costs by implementing innovative preventive care and health programs. The HealthPays program offers reduced rates for individuals with healthy life-styles. The organization's immunization and cancer-screening programs are nationally recognized. Group Health, the University of Washington, and Fred-Hutchinson Cancer Research Center work closely on a variety of programs, including teaching and research. Research priorities emphasize family health care, care for older adults, and clinical trials of intervention strategies.

Consumer governance sets Group Health apart from other health plans. A board of trustees elected by members ensures that consumers' concerns are addressed. A vote-by-mail process enables members to state their views

Eastside residents have become accustomed to Group Health's caring and concerned physicians. The organization has provided high-quality health care for three generations of Eastside families.

on important issues.

Group Health employees are active in a number of community-service efforts. The Foundation for Group Health Cooperative helped establish a community clinic in Bellevue, a support group for teenage parents, and an Eastside sexual assault center.

Group Health Cooperative is anticipating continued growth. Paramount to growth is the organization's commitment to providing affordable health maintenance treatment services to keep members healthy.

Photo by Gary Greene

13
THE MARKETPLACE

The Eastside's retail establishments and service industries are enjoyed by residents and visitors alike.

Photo by Gary Greene

BELLEVUE SQUARE

Bellevue Square is among the Eastside's most recognized tourist attractions. Each year more than 11 million people shop, browse, and dine at the mall's 200 shops, 4 department stores, and 17 restaurants. Recognized as the Northwest's premier shopping center, Bellevue Square was the first shopping center of its kind to be built in the Pacific Northwest.

Located in the heart of downtown Bellevue, Bellevue Square is a two-level shopping center built on 34 acres. An average of 30,000 people visit the mall daily, and the center employs approximately 3,000 full- and part-time people. Christmastime traffic is upwards of 70,000 per day. With 1.3 million square feet, the mall is classified as a super-regional shopping center. Bellevue Square has 5,034 park-

A jewel in the crown of the central court, Bellevue Square's 65-foot clocktower serves as a landmark meeting place for friends and family. Its clockworks and 1,500-pound bell were brought to Bellevue Square from a small town in Mississippi.

ing spaces and is anchored by four major department stores: Nordstrom, Frederick & Nelson, The Bon, and JCPenney.

Unique to Bellevue Square is the Bellevue Art Museum. Elevating oneself to some of the Northwest's finest art and crafts is as simple as taking Bellevue Square's glass elevator to the third floor. The museum, sponsored by the Pacific Northwest Arts and Crafts Association, was founded in 1975 as a result of dedicated work by community volunteers. It flourishes as one of the nation's few art museums located in a shopping center. The museum rents its 12,000 square feet from the Bellevue Square managers for one dollar per year. The arrangement has been a drawing card for both organizations, and community spirit and cooperation prevail.

Bellevue Square often serves as the town square for community events. For example, the Pacific Northwest Arts and Crafts Fair got its start at the mall. Bellevue Square was built for community interests as well as for shopping. The Overlake Thrift Shop and the Panaca Gallery are located within the center, both operating from space that is donated by the Bellevue Square Managers, Inc.

Bellevue Square also offers space for a number of other char-

Between residents and tourists, 11 million people shop, browse, and dine each year at Bellevue Square's 200 shops, 4 department stores, and 17 restaurants.

ity fund raisers, such as those for the American Cancer Society, Crimestoppers, and the Northwest Kidney Foundation. The Bellevue Square Managers Inc., in one night's event, raised more than $105,000 for 13 Eastside charities. A Night in New York provided funding equal to one-third of the human services budget for the entire city of Bellevue's budget.

Bellevue Square's impact on the region has been and continues to be significant. With the establishment of the center in 1946, Bellevue's downtown has flourished. The facility's sales exceed $350 million annually.

Construction on the facility began in 1945, eight years before the city was incorporated. Developer/owner Kemper Freeman, Sr., conducted a nationwide fact-finding tour of the nation's 22 existing regional shopping centers. Freeman patterned the center around Highland Park Village, a shopping center in Dallas. The original development plan was to obtain the most exposure of stores to parking fronts and to have a complete vari-

Mature trees and numerous other plantings enhance Bellevue Square with an open-air ambience.

ety of merchandise and services. The Bellevue Square first opened in 1946 with 16 stores, including Frederick & Nelson.

JCPenney opened in 1958. The 1960s was marked by more stores and the expansion of existing ones. Nordstrom, a local shoe store, was rebuilt in 1966 and became a major apparel store, increasing its square footage from 6,000 to 78,000. By 1970 the center had 50 stores, occupying more than 450,000 square feet.

The 1970s marked a period of remodeling and a remixing of merchants. Grocery stores, pharmacies, and hardware stores moved out and were replaced by smaller, higher-volume retailers. In 1980 a $100-million redevelopment effort was initiated. Built entirely by private funding, Bellevue Square is the only nonsubsidized downtown urban redevelopment of a regional shopping center built in the country in many years. Existing shopping center buildings became a contemporary, enclosed, multilevel structure with its own parking garage. Nordstrom and JCPenney were relocated to new buildings to serve as north and south anchors. Today the redeveloped Bellevue Square is the first enclosed, multilevel regional shopping center in the Puget Sound.

A major feature of the redeveloped mall is its concept of a European street scene, featuring 30- to 40-foot mature trees in three major mall courts, and three-dimensional storefronts, projecting up to three feet into the mall. Each storefront is constructed of different colors, designs, and building materials to create a jewelbox effect. The court and mall ceilings rise to a peak and are topped by skylights and extend the entire length of the mall. The central court, commonly referred to as a town square, contains a 65-foot-tall clock tower that also serves as a stairway between mall levels.

Bellevue Square also preserves much of what was evident from the original one-level open-air square. Old, familiar landmarks include architect George Wrede's Wishing Well, which was built as a charity fund raiser for the Children's Orthopedic Hospital. The *Forest Deity*, created by sculptor Dudley Carter, is an axe-hewn 12-foot wooden figure depicting a forest spirit. A community landmark, the sculpture now reigns over the northeast corner of Bellevue Square.

In more than 40 years Bellevue Square has become the region's foremost shopping area, offering a blend of small boutiques, excellent restaurants, and department stores and providing shoppers with an experience that can not be duplicated in the Pacific Northwest.

A special blend of shops and restaurants, coupled with the Bellevue Art Museum, make Bellevue Square a truly unique shopping experience.

RED LION HOTEL

The opening of the Red Lion Hotel in January 1982 was a signal to the community that Bellevue had finally arrived. The elaborately appointed hotel featured 355 luxury rooms, 18,000 square feet of meeting space, and two fine restaurants, all firsts for the community.

Bellevue was now a city to be reckoned with—a place in which out-of-towners could receive first-class hotel accommodations, a place in which residents and businesses could gather for large meetings and parties, and a place in which residents could enjoy fine dining and entertainment without having to drive across the bridge.

The opening of the Red Lion Hotel in Bellevue was also a milestone for the Red Lion owners. The positive acceptance the hotel received from the community convinced the chain's management

Business and leisure travelers have come to expect the ultimate in service and accommodations at Bellevue's Red Lion Hotel.

that it could successfully develop larger hotels in larger communities.

The hotel chain started as Red Lion and Thunderbird Inns in 1959 in Portland. In 26 years partners Todd McClaskey and Ed Pietz built 52 hotels throughout Oregon, Washington, Idaho, Montana, Nevada, and Northern California. In 1986 the partners sold their controlling interests to a new organization called Red Lion Acquisition Company.

The sale brought in new management, new money, and new growth. Today the firm owns and manages 53 properties, and three new hotels are under construction. The company projects it will add as many as five properties per

year for the next few years. Currently most of the growth is eastward into Colorado and Utah, and a lot of emphasis is also being given to properties in Southern California.

Through the years Red Lion Hotels & Inns has developed a loyal following among Northwest business travelers. Larger-than-average rooms and a good reputation for food and beverage have helped the chain, but management attributes most of the success to service.

"It seems as if everybody has rediscovered the idea that if you want to maintain your business, it's got to be based on service," says Steve Lindburg, general manager of the Bellevue Red Lion Hotel. "Red Lion has insisted on that since the beginning. It was hammered into us as employees, as mid-managers, and now as top

managers. Guest satisfaction is the goal."

As a matter of fact, Red Lion's goal is and always has been customer return. New business is great and good, especially in new areas, but the chain keys on retaining existing business.

Red Lion Hotels & Inns began as relatively major properties in small communities. Only in the past 10 years did management consider building larger properties in larger communities. The Bellevue property is the result of this newer approach.

"The two partners had a knack for choosing locations, and they saw the potential in Bellevue," says Lindburg. "They anticipated the more difficult commute, the growth in business, and rising property rates. This hotel was built to attract the corporate traveler and the group and association meeting business."

The Red Lion Hotel brought to Bellevue a new level of expectation and sophistication. The hotel gave the community a place to meet. Prior to the its opening, the largest ballroom was about 4,000 square feet. The Red Lion in Bellevue boasts a 10,000-square-foot ballroom and a total of 18,000 square feet of meeting space.

"The Red Lion came into town and took the image of motels and lodging up a notch," says Lindburg. "The hotel has been a boon to Bellevue, and Bellevue has been a boon to the hotel. The property has been successful since the day it opened."

Two fine dining establishments offer meals to satisfy the palates of discriminating epicurians.

The hotel employs 320 people and maintains one of the highest occupancy rates and also one of the highest rate structures of all the hotels in the chain. Although competition has increased, the hotel has not had to cut prices or cut services.

Lindburg has been very active with the local convention and visitors bureau and is on the committee assigned to design and critique the new convention center. In addition, he has found a way to host various charity and non-profit association events, including Boys and Girls Club auctions, chamber dinners, and Junior League functions. The hotel has been known to cut its margins significantly, virtually giving away its space, to give organizations the opportunity to hold their events, raise dollars, or celebrate accomplishments.

Of all the hotel's attributes, Lindburg is most pleased with the food and beverage service, including the restaurants on the property. For years hotel restaurants have been viewed unfavorably, but Red Lion made a commitment years ago to serve the best-possible food.

"Today a full 30 percent of our total revenue is food and beverage related," Lindburg says. "We chose to look at this as a profit center, as well as the opportunity to have local residents be our guests."

Misty's seats about 120 and caters to the fine dining experience. The Atrium Cafe features more casual dining. There are also two lounges, one with two dance floors, and the other a quiet bar that gives guests the opportunity to relax and converse.

Again and again, Lindburg points to service as the key to the Red Lion Hotel and Inn's success. Even though the hotel no longer can be distinguished as the only luxury hotel in Bellevue, it can still offer the best to its guests. Says Lindburg, "Our success hinges on meeting people's needs, following up on their requests, and making them feel as comfortable as possible until they get home."

Comfortable and elegantly appointed rooms provide rest and relaxation at the end of a full day.

SKIPPER'S, INC.

Despite intense competition and tight profit margins, Bellevue's Skipper's, Inc., has secured a spot in the fickle fast-food arena. For 20 years Puget Sound residents have enjoyed Skipper's fish and chips, shrimp, clams, seafood salads, and the chowder that has made the restaurant chain famous.

The chain was founded in 1969 by Herb Rosen, and the first restaurant was opened in downtown Bellevue. It was called Salty's Fish and Chips, but the name eventually was changed to Skipper's Seafood 'n Chowder House. The fish and chips menu was well received locally, and by 1971 expansion plans were under way.

Today the company employs 3,000 and has sales of more than $100 million annually. The state's largest restaurant corporation, Skipper's restaurants may be found in more than 216 locations throughout the western United States and Canada. Of that total, 185 are company owned and operated, and the balance are run by franchise agreements.

Patrons receive cooked-to-order meals that cost from three dollars to $4.80. Positioned at the upper end of the fast-food market,

Friendly faces and fast service ensure that the customer is number one at Skipper's.

the restaurants do 40 percent of their business at lunch and 60 percent at dinner, contrary to most fast-food chains.

Skipper's management maintains that the company is customer driven, and employees are taught that the customer is number one. Skipper's president Everett "Jeff" Jefferson says the firm's success can be attributed to four operating goals: to create value for the customer, to create profit and return on investment for shareholders, to create an exciting work place for employees, and to be fair to suppliers.

A publicly owned company, Skipper's has recently restructured into a leaner management that is closer to operations.

New emphasis has been placed on research and development involving both permanent and short-term menu items.

Seafood lovers in Bellevue know that Skipper's is the place for tasty, cooked-to-order fish and chips.

Skipper's is also testing such concepts as drive-up service and has successfully tested take-out packaging alternatives and service systems.

Jefferson initiated a $7-million interior and exterior remodel/redecorating program. Close to $50,000 will be spent per restaurant, and the effort will take about three years to complete. Brown and rust tones are being replaced with grays, blues, and reds that give a fresher, cleaner look.

Innovative employee recruitment and retention programs have helped the company attract conscientious and dedicated young people and senior citizens. There have also been successful scholarship programs and programs aimed at disabled and handicapped persons. Because the restaurants serve wine and beer, Skipper's employees are older than at most fast-food chains, averaging 25 years of age.

Skipper's has established active community relations programs in all the areas it serves. It strives to be considered a hometown business.

Indicative of Skipper's customer-driven attitude is the designation by *Restaurants and Institutions Magazine* as a "Choice in Chains." Customers rated Skipper's a good value with superb food.

BELLEVUE PLACE

Opened in 1988, Bellevue Place represents many firsts for the Pacific Northwest. In downtown Bellevue adjacent to Bellevue Square, the $160-million multiuse project includes a 24-story luxury hotel, a 21-story office tower, a 6-story office and retail complex centered around an atrium, and a 17-acre, five-story underground parking garage.

The region's first true mixed-use center, the project includes the 382-room Hyatt Regency Hotel that was designed by Wimberley Allison Tonag & Goo of Los Angeles. The luxury hotel features nine conference rooms, several elaborate ballrooms, a piano lounge, and Eques, a fine restaurant.

Bellevue Place provides a state-of-the-art working environment for more than 2,000 people. Almost every floor of the 21-story Seafirst Tower offers spectacular views of the Cascade and Olympic mountain ranges. Seafirst Bank is located in the lobby of the building that was designed to create a higher number of corner offices on each floor. Public spaces invite use as a civic center for the performing arts.

Plenty of space for high-end gourmet and specialty shops has been planned, and street-level arcades with large display windows invite passersby to shop at luxury retail stores. Men and women's clothing, fine jewelry and accessories, a camera store, a bookstore, and an art gallery are located within the complex. Development plans include a performing arts center and a deluxe condominium tower.

A project of Kemper Development Company of Bellevue, Bellevue Place was built by a group of general partners that includes Bellevue Place Properties, C. Itoh & Company Limited, Konoike Construction Company Limited, Itogumi Construction Company Limited, Seafirst Bank, Davis Wright and Jones, Baugh Construction Company, J.C. Investment & Realty, and Hyatt Hotels. Baugh Construction Company of Seattle was the general contractor for the complex. The master plan and office buildings were designed by Kober/Sclater Associates of Seattle.

Bellevue Place comprises

A 24-story hotel, a 21-story office tower, and a 6-story office and retail complex all integrate perfectly as parts of Bellevue Place, the Eastside's premier urban activity center.

The gracefully styled Wintergarden lets gentle light fall upon Bellevue Place tenants and visitors.

three main structures: the hotel and officer towers and a six-story office and retail complex that houses the Seattle Club, a premier health club. The Wintergarden, a six-story atrium with approximately 11,000 square feet of space for small shops on two levels, adjoins Seafirst Building and the Eques restaurant. When complete, Bellevue Place will house more than 30 shops and restaurants.

An urban activity center, Bellevue Place provides a beautiful environment in which both residents and visitors can feel comfortable in the most modern and secure buildings ever constructed in the region. Bellevue Place truly is a place in which every tenant's needs were anticipated before moving in. Developer Kemper Freeman, Jr., built the Bellevue Place with a general goal that it would be a place of which all Bellevue could be proud and that it would be a place for people.

RESIDENCE INN BY MARRIOTT, BELLEVUE

A hotel is a place to stay, but the Residence Inn by Marriott, Bellevue, is a place to live—whether guests spend the night, a week, or a month.

Guests may enjoy the comforts of home and receive the services of a hotel at the 120-suite complex just off I-520 in Bellevue. Twice the size of most hotel rooms, Residence Inn suites are beautifully appointed "homes away from home," complete with sleeping, dining, and living areas. Three floor plans—studio, executive, and penthouse—are furnished for the ultimate in comfort and practicality for relocating families, traveling businesspeople, and discriminating vacationers.

The Residence Inn concept was the original idea of businessman Jack DeBoer of Wichita, Kansas. DeBoer was developing an apartment complex that would be worth $1,800 per month for rent, but was denied financing on the grounds that renters would find the residence unaffordable. Forced to restrategize, DeBoer considered that $1,800 was equal to $60 per night for one month—a reasonable rate for extended hotel visits. The astute developer approached his financers once again, this time with

The ultimate in comfort and practicality is to be found at the Residence Inn by Marriott, Bellevue, designed for guests who expect the comfort of home.

the idea of using the building as a deluxe hotel for extended visits. His plan won their approval, and the first Residence Inn was built in 1974.

Basically DeBoer was pursuing the extended-stay market—travelers who are relocating, training, or conducting business for more than one or two nights. Today almost 60 percent of Residence Inn business is made up of extended-stay travelers.

Travelers who stay fewer than four nights comprise 40 percent of Residence Inn business. These travelers prefer the accommodations and services of the Residence Inn over those of a conventional hotel. In 10 years DeBoer built and franchised some 100 Residence Inns nationwide. Opened five years ago, the Residence Inn, Bellevue, has enjoyed better than an 80-percent occupancy rate annually. It is among the chain's most profitable properties.

In July 1987 Marriott Corp. bought Residence Inns nationwide. Marriott, an internationally respected hospitality company, has discovered a growing market for this concept. The firm expects to more than triple the number of Residence Inn locations nationwide by the 1990s.

"The idea is for a sense of community, of town house-style suites for travelers looking for a full range of conveniences," according to Bill Marriott, chairman and president of Marriott Corp.

While some Residence Inns are owned and managed by Marriott, most are owned by franchise companies. The Residence Inn, Bellevue, is one of six properties in the Pacific Northwest owned and oper-

Much more than a place to hang one's hat, each suite has beautifully and thoroughly appointed kitchen, bedroom, and living room areas.

ated by InnVentures, Inc., in Seattle, Washington. Larry Culver, president of InnVentures and a Northwest native, is researching sites for new locations throughout the West and plans to add 20 new Residence Inns during the next five years.

Each Residence Inn is managed and operated like a small business. Each Residence Inn manager is responsible for staffing, maintenance, and, most important, assuring that guests receive the best in service and amenities.

The Residence Inn, Bellevue, is the epitome of excellence when it comes to service. Testament to this is a bulging "scrap book" in the inn's elegant Gatehouse. The book contains some 200 letters from chief executive officers, civic leaders, and citizens throughout

Nets and hoops await the tennis or basketball enthusiast at the fully equipped sports court.

the area and the nation who have stayed at the Residence Inn, Bellevue. These letters thank the staff for its warmth and helpfulness, and commend the facility for its interior design, on-site amenities, and community support and involvement.

Guest activities, large suites with fully equipped kitchens, coin-operated laundry facilities, complimentary grocery shopping, in-room VCRs, and a FAX machine are a few of the specialized services and amenities that the Residence Inn, Bellevue, offers that most hotels do not. Homey extras in each suite include popcorn and a popcorn popper, coffee ready to be brewed, and logs in the fireplace.

Residence Inns also offer most conventional hotel services, including a sports court with equipment, 24-hour front desk service, maid service, airport transportation, and a conference room with audiovisual and catering capabilities. The Residence Inns' $70- to $159-per-night rates compare with and often beat those of full-service hotels.

Weekly and seasonal guest activities are geared to weary business travelers and to relocating families with young children. On Tuesday evenings, guests are invited to the Gatehouse to join the manager and the staff for cocktails and hors d'oeuvres. On Saturday mornings, kids are invited to the Gatehouse to view children's movies. The staff hosts a Christmas tree trimming and holiday party, a Fourth of July picnic complete with hot dogs and apple pie, and other seasonal events throughout the year.

As well, the Residence Inn, Bellevue, is committed to the Eastside community, supporting and participating in the Bellevue Philharmonic, the Bellevue Chamber of Commerce, and the East King County Convention and Visitors' Bureau. The manager believes a hotel needs to be actively involved in the community it serves and that it should be a part of the community's decision-making process.

Community service activities are ongoing at the Residence Inn, Bellevue. The inn provides Christmas for a needy family. Gifts, food, complimentary two-day lodging, and a Christmas tree with all the trimmings are donated. The effort is well received by the family and by the staff. "These efforts benefit the community and they benefit the inn," general manager Gary Tachiyama says. "We get a lot of referrals because of our attitude toward community service."

A newspaper travel editor summed up her stay at the Residence Inn, Bellevue: "A new and welcome concept in the hotel world . . . the concept combines hotel and home amenities . . . the staff is delightful and accommodating . . . the appeal is wide."

Rustic wood decks connecting the suites provide an air of relaxation.

PATRONS

The following individuals, companies, and organizations have made a valuable commitment to the quality of this publication. Windsor Publications and the Bellevue Chamber of Commerce gratefully acknowledge their participation in *Bellevue and the New Eastside.*

Accountants Microsystems, Inc.
Bellevue Community College
Bellevue Place
Bellevue Square
Boeing Computer Services
Borden Chemical
CH2M HILL
P.S. Clark, Nuber and Co.
Dain Bosworth Inc.
First Mutual Bank
Foster Pepper & Shefelman
Group Health Cooperative of
   Puget Sound
HNTB
The Journal American
Key Bank of Puget Sound
KLSY Radio
Lake Washington Vocational
   Technical Institute
Lease Crutcher Lewis

Microsoft Corporation
Mithun Partners
Overlake Hospital Medical Center
PACCAR Inc
KPMG Peat Marwick
Penwest
Puget Sound Power & Light
   Company
Quadrant Corporation
Red Lion Hotel
Residence Inn by Marriott,
   Bellevue
Revelle, Ries & Hawkins
SDL Corporation
Seafirst Bank
Security Pacific Bank
Skipper's, Inc.
Sweeney Conrad
United Olympic Life Insurance
   Company
Viacom Cable
Washington Natural Gas
Wilsey & Ham Pacific, Inc.

Participants in Part Two, "Eastside Enterprises." The stories of these companies and organizations appear in Chapters 8 through 13, beginning on page 116.

BIBLIOGRAPHY

BOOKS

Ely, Arline. *Our Foundering Fathers.* Kirkland, Wash.: Kirkland Public Library, 1975.

Fish, Edwards R. *The Past at Present.* N.p., 1967.

Johnston, Helen and Richard. *Willowmoor.* Redmond, Wash.: King County Historical Association, 1976.

Karolevitz, Robert F. *Kemper Freeman Sr. and the Bellevue Story.* Mission Hill, S.D.: The Homestead Publishers, 1984.

McDonald, Lucile. *Bellevue: Its First 100 Years.* Bellevue, Wash.: Friends of the Bellevue Library, 1984.

Phillips, James W. *Washington State Place Names.* Seattle: University of Washington Press, 1971.

Squires, Betty Jo. *Bellevue Story.* N.p., 1967.

Warren, James R. *King County and Its Queen City: Seattle.* Northridge, Calif.: Windsor Publications, Inc., 1981.

Whyte, William H. *City: Rediscovering the Center.* New York: Doubleday, 1989.

NEWSPAPERS

Daily Journal of Commerce
The Journal American
Seattle Post-Intelligencer
Seattle Times

ADDITIONAL RESOURCES

Bellevue Chamber of Commerce
Bellevue Downtown Association
Bellevue Library
Bothell Chamber of Commerce
Bothell Library
East King County Convention & Visitors Bureau
Issaquah Chamber of Commerce
King County Department of Parks, Planning and Resources
Kirkland Chamber of Commerce
Kirkland Library
Puget Sound Council of Governments
Redmond Chamber of Commerce
Redmond Library
Seattle-King County Economic Development Council

INDEX